ASK THEM WHY

ASK THEM WHY

How to Help Unbelievers Find the Truth

Jay Lucas

REGULAR BAPTIST PRESS
1300 North Meacham Road
Schaumburg, Illinois 60173

DEDICATION

*I have always been surrounded by people I do
not deserve: my beloved wife, Becky, and six
wonderful children—Sharayah, Courtney,
Jonathan, Trinity, Rebekah, and Kirsten;
professors and teachers who taught me to love
God's Word; and a staff and church family
at Grace Community Baptist Church, which
are second to none.*

This book includes two audio CDs of the encounters in part 2. If you are
using this book in a group setting, listen to the audio CD as a group before
you read the analysis and discuss the questions that follow each printed encounter. If you are using the book outside a class setting, you will profit, as
well, by listening to the encounter before you read the analysis and questions.

ASK THEM WHY
© 2007 Regular Baptist Press • Schaumburg, Illinois
www.RegularBaptistPress.org • 1-800-727-4440
All rights reserved. Printed in U.S.A.
RPB5356 • ISBN: 978-1-59402-250-0

Third Printing—2011

CONTENTS

APPENDIXES

FOREWORD

Proclaim the truth. Defend the truth.
Embrace genuine truth claims.
Expose false truth claims.

THIS book, *Ask Them Why*, will help you to do just that. It will provide a process whereby you can distinguish truth from error (1 John 4:1–6), contend for the faith of evangelical Christianity (Jude 3), and proclaim the inerrant Word of God (2 Tim. 4:2).

Jay Lucas is a loving husband, a guiding parent, and a faithful pastor of a growing congregation. He served as my associate pastor for three years before I retired as senior pastor. It was my joy to recommend him to the deacons and to the church as my successor.

In addition, Jay is both an apologist and an evangelist. He is aware of the deception of the contemporary postmodern culture and its impact upon both believers and nonbelievers. He has confronted its proponents both by spoken word and written form. However, he doesn't want just to win an argument; he engages postmodernists in compassion to bring them to redemption through Jesus Christ.

Many Christians know *what* they believe, but they cannot explain *why*. Thus they are timid in their outreach to the lost. This book is not for the fainthearted or for the weak-minded. It will stretch you—your thinking, your faith, and your vocabulary comprehension. This book will encourage you to become a stronger, more informed child of God.

It is my prayer that you will develop a Biblical worldview and that you will articulate it to an unredeemed world. *Ask Them Why* will guide you in this pursuit. I highly recommend it to all believers who want to grow in grace and in the knowledge of Jesus Christ (2 Pet. 3:18).

Dr. Robert Gromacki
Pastor Emeritus, Grace Community Baptist Church
Distinguished Professor Emeritus
of Bible and Greek, Cedarville University

INTRODUCTION

IT IS my honor and privilege to be able to commend to you this first published work of my friend and mentor, Pastor Jay Lucas. God has gifted me with Jay's friendship for over twenty years, and as fellow pastors we have had numerous discussions relating to the need for believers to be adequately equipped to defend their faith ("apologetics") and the most Scriptural approach for doing so. During my doctoral program, it was my privilege to be able to serve alongside Jay in pastoral ministry in upstate New York, and it was during those years that the book you now hold first began to take shape. While numerous books are available on Christian apologetics, there are three reasons why this work should be highly commended to the Christian public.

First, unlike most books on apologetics, which are written by professional theologians or "ivory tower" scholars, this book is preeminently *pastoral*, which is seen in a number of ways. For example, it seeks to equip everyday believers for the ministry of winning their lost friends to Christ (Eph. 4:11, 12). And it exudes a spirit of graciousness (Col. 4:6) consistent with the heart of a pastor who understands through years of ministry that it is more important to win a soul to Christ through the unleashed power of the Word of God (Rom. 10:17) than it is to win a cleverly crafted argument. This book also differs from other works on Christian apologetics in that it is eminently *readable*. Anyone who has attempted to wade through the existing literature on Christian apologetics will tell you what a blessing this book is.

As a professor, I have been waiting years for a book such as this one. Its readability not only makes it useful for the busy pastor, but—more importantly—accessible to laypeople who would never get past the first chapter of other apologetics books. If one of the marks of genuine scholarship is the ability to take complex subjects and arguments and present them clearly and simply so that normal people can understand them, then this book represents a remarkable piece of scholarship. Jay possesses that rare (and enviable) gift of writing with conciseness and brevity without sacrificing content or substance in the process. Endnotes provide resources for further study for the reader whose appetite has been stimulated.

Second, this book is *presuppositional.* In our discussions over the years, Jay and I have been guided by a presuppositional approach to apologetics, largely because, of all the apologetical systems, it takes the theological realities of the depravity of mankind and the absolute authority of Scripture most seriously. Furthermore, presuppositionalism recognizes that *everyone*—believers and unbelievers alike—operates from a set of assumptions that greatly influences how he handles the evidence. This book builds off the premise that most unbelievers have never considered the implications of their own presuppositions and where they inevitably lead.

A third reason why this book represents a valuable addition to the existing literature on Christian apologetics is that it is eminently *practical.* Again, most apologetics books are primarily theoretical, and certainly good practice must have good theory as its basis. However, most apologetics books seem to stop there. They provide little help in showing the believer what Christian apologetics looks like in real life. Once again, this book fills that gap with the real-life scenarios that make up the bulk of the work. I am aware of no other published work on Christian apologetics that includes a section like Part 2: Encounters. These scenarios alone are worth the price of the book. *Ask Them Why* gives believers equipment to interact effectively with *real* people who hold such views and enables believers to be prepared ahead of time to channel the conversation to the gospel. (This is especially valuable for people like me who don't think fast on their feet!)

The common denominator in each of these cases is the effective use of questions that invariably compel unbelievers to face the implications of their own presuppositions. Given how often Jesus, Paul, and the Old Testament prophets used questions to persuade their listeners, it is amazing how often this approach is overlooked in books on Christian apologetics. *Ask Them Why* goes a long way to fill that gap.

For these reasons and more, I am delighted to be able to recommend this book to you. I join my friend the author in praying that this work will serve as a valuable tool in equipping believers everywhere to "always [be] ready to make a defense [the Greek word is *apologia*] to everyone who asks you to give an account for the hope that is in you, yet with gentleness and reverence" (1 Pet. 3:15, NASB). *Soli Deo Gloria!*

> *Michael M. Canham, ThM, PhD*
> *Professor of Theology and Bible Exposition*
> *The Cornerstone Seminary, Vallejo, California*

PREFACE

THE typical non-Christian is even less prepared to defend his beliefs than is the typical Christian! This realization plays a major role in this book. If an unbeliever resists the gospel when we share it with him, it is because he is relying on something other than God for determining the meaning and purpose of life, as well as for discovering truth itself. That person's belief system, whatever it is, is false and logically self-defeating. The probability is that the person has never had this fact pointed out to him. I pray that after reading this book, you will understand the value of asking the unbeliever to explain the reasons for his beliefs. I also pray that this book will help you learn to dissect unbelief and expose it as error.

The first section of this book explains the methodology that I call the Ask Them Why (ATW) approach. The second section comprises fictional encounters between non-Christians and Christians who use the ATW method. At the end of each encounter is a summary to help the reader identify the key points made by the Christian. There are also several appendixes after the encounter section. I suggest reading each appendix the first time it is referred to, whether in the main body of the book or in the endnotes. The ATW method is not the only way to share the gospel, but I think it is an approach that can be of great value for the believer and the unbeliever.

Another important fact needs to be acknowledged at the outset. Within scholarly Christian circles there is a complex debate regarding the proper approach to apologetics. Examining the debated issues is valuable, but such an evaluation is not the purpose of this book. In my own study of apologetics I have read dozens of books and journal articles, listened to numerous lectures by leading Christian apologists, and talked to some of them in person. I have observed these apologists in action as they have debated atheists, skeptics, and other non-Christians. Most importantly, I have searched the Scriptures to see for myself what method of defending and proclaiming the faith is most Biblical. My hope and desire is that this book honors the Lord of the Bible and that He will be pleased to use it both to encourage believers and to rescue unbelievers from spiritual darkness.

Part 1

THE

ASK
THEM
WHY

METHOD

GET INTO
THE GAME

MANY Christians find personal evangelism intimidating. They would rather give their last dollar to the missionary fund than to engage someone in a meaningful conversation about Jesus Christ, prompting an observer to question their depth of love for Him. After all, believers who truly love Jesus Christ will obey His commands, which include being His witnesses (Acts 1:8). Failure to do so indicates a lack of commitment.

This assessment might be true, yet it does not tell the whole story. Many Christians who are reluctant to witness are discouraged and shamed by their failure. If they did not love Christ, their silence would not bother them. The level of frustration and regret indicates that for many believers the problem is not a lack of love for Christ but a lack of confidence in their ability to effectively communicate the claims of Christ in an increasingly secular or post-Christian culture.[1]

I recall my struggle to witness to my friends when I was a student in a public high school. Connecticut was not even close to being a Bible Belt state, and my hometown was no exception. Our area had few Bible-believing, doctrinally sound churches, and those that existed had small youth groups at best. In a school of a thousand students, I knew of only three other born-again students. I assume there were more than the four of us, but if so, the others were as anonymous as I. I knew and believed the gospel, but I doubted my ability to explain it in a reasonable way to someone who was inclined to resist it. Today as I look back on those days, I find myself thinking, *If only I had known then what I know now. If someone had taught me how to defend my beliefs, I would have had the courage to speak up.*

This book has been written to help Christians of all ages and abilities proclaim and defend the claims of the gospel. The task is not as difficult as many Christians perceive. Those who have rejected Jesus Christ and the Bible are standing on shaky ground. In contrast, a trained Christian has every reason to be confident in his or her position.

Because I am a pastor, I feel especially burdened to encourage Christians and to help them learn to defend their Christian beliefs. Although Christians in America don't face the kind of violent persecution found in other parts of the world, they are still under attack in the arena of ideas. Over the years I have heard too many accounts of Christian teens going off to colleges and universities only to have their faith completely undermined. When I have had occasion to speak with such students, I invariably discover that they have fallen prey to weak and easily rebutted arguments against the Bible and Christianity. How much better it would have been had they been taught apologetics in their home churches. Too often we are merely shutting the barn door after the horse has run off.

It is not just college students who need to be equipped.

Every Christian is commanded to be ready to give an answer when asked about the Christian faith (1 Pet. 3:15). If every Christian attended a Biblically sound seminary or Christian college, the local church would be far better prepared to engage the larger culture in which we live.

The reality is that only a small percentage of Christians attend such educational institutions. To make matters worse, many students who attend Christian colleges for four years never actually take an apologetics course.[2] As a result, our churches are filled with people who love the Lord and care about lost people yet are unprepared to answer attacks against the Christian faith.

I believe we need to take apologetics to the streets; the use of apologetics should be made practical enough that we can actually use it as a tool in our daily interaction. To do this we must teach it in our churches. Defending the Christian faith does not need to be a losing battle. The more that Christians begin to understand the strength of the Christian belief system, the more we will see Christians emboldened to share their faith.

Before proceeding, an important truth needs to be stated. The power of salvation resides in the gospel message itself (Rom. 1:16; Heb. 4:12; 2 Tim. 3:15). Even as a timid high school student, I could have been an effective witness for Christ by sharing the gospel in spite of not being equipped to defend my beliefs. God changes hearts through His Word by the power of the Holy Spirit (Titus 3:5). This transaction does not depend on our debating skills (1 Cor. 2:1–5). Therefore, this book does not proceed from the premise that the lost will remain unconverted unless we master certain logical arguments.

This book builds on the premise that Christians should take the necessary steps to become better trained as servants for God's use as we grow in our knowledge of Him. Learning to articulate the superiority of the Christian worldview over mankind's false systems provides great freedom and encouragement.[3] This mastery can greatly reduce the fear and anxiety sincere Christians often experience when witnessing. Reservations can be replaced by excitement and confidence, resulting in rich blessing for the Christian as he joyfully seeks to fulfill the Great Commission (Matt. 28:18–20).

An additional benefit awaits the Christian who strives to sharpen his skills for God's use. I have found that as I increase my studying, my confidence in the reliability of the Scriptures and my walk with Christ have become more vibrant. Yes, I am now more confident to share Christ with non-Christians than I was during my youth, but I also personally enjoy the Christian life more than I had ever thought possible. The process of examining my beliefs, comparing them to non-Christian beliefs, and learning to defend my beliefs has been the single greatest source of growth and blessing in my life.

The field of apologetics is undergoing significant changes that correspond to the rise of postmodernism. Many Christian thinkers believe that traditional apologetics is in danger of becoming irrelevant in a postmodern culture, which has little use for logic and propositional truth. Some of the concerns of these Christian thinkers are valid and need to be incorporated into twenty-first-century apologetics. On the other hand, I believe that some of the concerns amount to little more than nervous hand-wringing that minimizes the power of God's truth to overcome error and unbelief. Ask Them Why (ATW) reflects an awareness that postmodernism, a dominant worldview, must be addressed (see appendix D, page 239). We Christians can be confident that God's truth will stand the test of time and that whenever the next major paradigm shift occurs (post-postmodernism!), the gospel of Jesus Christ will still be rescuing the hearts and minds of men and women, boys and girls.

Appendix C (p. 225) presents a partial transcript of a formal debate in which I participated. In some ways the debate represented the culmination of my studies in apologetics. When I was in high school, I would not have believed someone who told me I would someday debate the existence of God in such a setting. The experience was exceptionally positive, and it strengthened my belief that almost any Christian who is willing to think through the issues can learn how to effectively proclaim and defend the gospel. Christian, let's do our homework, prepare our hearts in prayer, and then get into the game.

Notes

1. By "secular" I do not necessarily mean crass naturalism or atheism (although this is included). Tens of millions of Americans claim to believe in God, yet this professed belief does not govern their actions in their daily lives. To those people who claim belief in God but rarely give it much thought, I attach the label "secular." By "post-Christian" I mean the growing trend in our culture to move away from the Christian underpinnings of early American history. Unlike in the past, a high percentage of Americans today have never been exposed to the Bible and are completely unaware of even its most basic teachings.

2. For those who want a comprehensive treatment of the various methods of apologetics and an introduction to dozens of individual apologists, I recommend *Faith Has Its Reasons: An Integrative Approach to Defending Christianity* by Kenneth Boa and Robert M. Bowman, Jr. (Colorado Springs: NavPress, 2001).

3. Everyone has a worldview. The term "worldview" refers to a person's core beliefs, which provide him or her with a "lens" through which the person sees and interprets the world and his or her place in it. Many people are not fully aware of their worldview commitments, but this lack of awareness does not prevent them from making use of their worldviews. This book will teach the Christian how to expose the flaws of non-Christian worldviews. A worldview includes a belief about God's existence and His character, standards of right and wrong, the nature of reality, and the meaning of life, among other essentials. The right-thinking Christian bases his or her worldview on the truths revealed in the inerrant Scripture. Appendix A (p. 209) is a fuller explanation of the Christian worldview.

CHAPTER I

THE POWER OF QUESTIONS

"WHERE are you?" This simple question is one of the most profound and important ever asked. It was the question God asked Adam after Adam and Eve sinned and hid from Him in the Garden of Eden (Gen. 3:6-9). Didn't God know? He did. He asked this question and the ones that followed, not for His information but for Adam and Eve's benefit (Gen. 3:11-13). God's questions forced the couple to acknowledge truths they did not want to face.

Questions: A Powerful Tool

A well-conceived question or series of questions can be a powerful tool in the proclamation and defense of the truth. Most Christians recognize the importance of proclaiming and defending the truth, but many have little understanding of, or appreciation for, the value of questions. This situation exists even though the Bible is saturated with questions posed to expose the truth already known to the questioner. Christians who learn to effectively duplicate the Biblical model will find that evangelism and apologetics need not be a cause for fear and timidity but an act of courage, boldness, and confidence. The Ask Them Why (ATW) method is fairly easy to master. It cannot be mastered, however, until it is first understood.

Jesus: The Master Questioner

The Master Questioner in the Scriptures was Jesus Christ. In Matthew 14:31—17:25 Jesus asked almost two dozen questions, and because He is omniscient, He knew the answer to every one of them. Why then did He ask them? He asked questions to reveal a great deal of truth to the person who answered the questions.[1]

Jesus frequently asked His disciples questions. He also dealt with unbelievers in a similar manner. Consider two examples. In Matthew 16:13 Christ asked His disciples, "Who do men say that I, the Son of Man, am?" Jesus perfectly knew the answer to that question. But He asked the question to sharpen the thinking of the men to whom He addressed the question. After they answered (v. 14), Jesus asked them a follow-up question: "But who do you say that I am?" (v. 15). The thinking prompted by Jesus' questions was important in the process of preparing the disciples for future ministry.

A second example of the value of questions is found in Matthew 22:41-46. Jesus asked the same type of questions He had asked the disciples in Matthew 16, but in this case Jesus was dealing with the unbelieving Pharisees. Again, Jesus demonstrated the power of a carefully crafted series of questions. Note that His opening question was similar to the one put to the disciples: "What do you think about the Christ? Whose Son is He?" (v. 42).

The Pharisees replied, "The Son of David" (v. 42). By giving this particular answer, the Pharisees revealed that they were failing to acknowledge the full implications of the person of Jesus, that is, His deity. He then asked a follow-up question by appealing to the Pharisees' own source of beliefs, the Old Testament. (The Pharisees at least claimed to be committed to the Scriptures, though in reality they did not truly practice them.) He asked, "How then does David in the Spirit call Him 'Lord'?" (v. 43). Jesus quoted Psalm 110:1 and asked the Pharisees, "If David then calls Him 'Lord,' how is He his Son?" (v. 45). Matthew recorded the response in verse 46: "And no one was able to answer Him a word, nor from that day on did anyone dare question Him anymore."

In this portion of Scripture, we see that Jesus exposed the errors of the Pharisees simply by asking questions. By their own errors they were reduced to silence. (See also Matthew 21:23–27.)

Our Goal: To Speak the Truth in Love

It would have been wonderful if, upon having their errors pointed out, the Pharisees had had an immediate change of heart and embraced Jesus as "the Christ" and the Son of God. We should desire that response for all unbelievers. However, there is another important goal too: rendering the arguments of unbelievers powerless. People may still cling to their errors, but let it be in spite of sound reasoning to the contrary. The apostle Paul expressed it in this way: "Casting down arguments and every high thing that exalts itself against the knowledge of God, bringing every thought into captivity to the obedience of Christ" (2 Cor. 10:5). We must rely on the Holy Spirit to touch the hearts of unbelievers, but let us fulfill our obligation to speak the truth and expose error.

This approach may include an attitude that the Christian must guard against. Our goal must not be to win an argument for the purpose of feeding our pride. It is not too difficult to trap most non-Christians with our questions because they hold views that are inherently defective. Our goal must always be to speak the truth in love (Eph. 4:15) and to acknowledge their lost condition and point them to the salvation found in Christ alone (Acts 4:12). As someone has said, sharing the gospel is like one beggar showing another beggar where to find bread. We ask unbelievers questions to help them see that they need bread and do not know where to find it. Then by the grace of God, we can show unbelievers that the bread they need is Jesus Christ, the Bread of Life (John 6:35).

If unbelievers continue to reject the truth after being shown the errors of their position and the supremacy of the Biblical worldview, we at least know that we have spoken the truth and opposed error. This is no small issue. Christians who seek to be Biblical must love the truth. We must desire to see people brought to the truth, but even if they reject the truth, we perform a sacred service when we proclaim and defend it.

The Method: Ask Them Why

What questions should we ask? What errors are we trying to expose? Part 2 presents fictional encounters between Christians and non-Christians. These encounters are designed to show that in our culture there is no shortage of opportunities to ask questions that lead to truth. Every thinking person has his own set of beliefs, some of which are true and some of which are false. The non-Christian holds even true beliefs without adequate reasons. The encounter scenarios in part 2 show that the only sound basis for knowing truth and believing truth is a surrender of intellectual autonomy and submission to the teachings of God's authoritative revelation to mankind.[2] This revelation is found in the Bible. The process begins when we ask an unbeliever, why?[3]

Notes

1. Jesus asked different types of questions for different reasons, depending on the issue and the audience. The parable of the Good Samaritan is an example (Luke 10:25-37). For our present purposes, let it simply be noted that Jesus regularly made use of questions in the proclamation of truth.

2. The concept of intellectual autonomy is an important one. "Autonomy" basically means "self-law," or "self-rule." Intellectual autonomy speaks of the human propensity to set one's self up as the highest or final authority when it comes to the question of truth. This propensity first appeared in the Garden of Eden when the serpent persuaded Eve to set up her own thinking as the ultimate standard (Gen. 3:1-6). Eve decided that God's word was not the highest authority and that it had to satisfy her sense of the way things ought to be. Over the centuries, intellectual autonomy has produced various forms of unbelief. The momentum today is toward postmodernism. (See appendix D, page 239.)

3. The Greek philosopher Socrates made use of questions as a method for exposing false assumptions and error as well as for planting seeds of truth or fleshing out truth that was innately known. Not surprisingly, his method became known as the Socratic method, but I do not believe that this Greek philosopher should be given credit as the originator of "the question as teaching tool." The ancient book of Job testifies that God Himself was unsurpassed as a questioner many centuries before Socrates was born (Job 38—41). Also, Socrates' view of innate knowledge differs from Biblical epistemology at key points, but that topic is beyond the scope of this volume.

For an interesting illustration of the Socratic method, I recommend Peter Kreeft's *Socrates Meets Jesus: History's Greatest Questioner Confronts the Claims of Christ* (Downers Grove, IL: InterVarsity Press, 1987). I strongly disagree with some of Kreeft's theology, but I have great respect for his abilities as a writer and thinker.

CHAPTER 2

WE LIVE IN ATHENS

S OMEDAY I would like to visit Athens, Greece. It is a city rich in history and culture. To walk its streets and explore its sites would be a memorable experience. Ideas that circulated there hundreds of years before Christ walked on the earth have left their mark on American political theory. But I think there is a far more important parallel between ancient Athens and contemporary America. Recognizing the parallel is vitally important for effectively sharing Jesus Christ and for using Ask Them Why (ATW).

What is the connection between Athens and America? In both settings, ignorance of the Bible and the Biblical worldview are evident. And now, as then, evangelism often needs to cover other ground before the conversation reaches the presentation of the Cross. Don't misunderstand; our goal is always to present the gospel, which is based upon the death and resurrection of Jesus Christ. But how we tell the gospel story depends on what the audience already knows or doesn't know.

The Gospel Presented to Jews

To help clarify the Athens-America comparison, let's journey back in time two thousand years and compare Athens to Jerusalem. The book of Acts is an exciting account of the birth of the New Testament church and the spread of the gospel. Where did it begin? In Jerusalem. In Acts 1:8 Jesus told His disciples that they would be His witnesses, first in Jerusalem and Judea, then in Samaria, and ultimately to the uttermost parts of the earth.

In Acts 2:14–41 we read the account of Peter's famous sermon on the Day of Pentecost. This was the first public presentation of the gospel after Jesus' ascension. This is also the event we use to mark the birth of the New Testament church. Peter was barely into his sermon when he began quoting the Hebrew Scriptures (our Old Testament). Peter quoted the prophet Joel and then two of David's psalms (Ps. 16; 110). By using these passages, Peter was able to quickly establish the claim that Jesus was the Messiah and that not only His death but also His resurrection were prophesied and ordained by God. The people listening to Peter were cut to the heart, and thousands repented and turned to Jesus Christ (Acts 2:37–41). What a way to start the church!

This powerful sermon was preached in Jerusalem to a Jewish audience. Why is that fact significant? Peter's Christian worldview and the Jewish worldview of his audience were virtually the same (other than the questions pertaining to Jesus of Nazareth). Both Peter and his listeners believed in the existence of God; that is, they believed that Jehovah is God. Both sides agreed that God had revealed Himself through the Scriptures. There was no question that Joel and Psalms are both God's Word. Everyone agreed that God is a God of miracles and that God had promised to send a Messiah. The concepts of sin, God's wrath, atonement, mercy, and resurrection were already held in common. In other words, the theological, philosophical, ethical, and historical groundwork was already in place. Peter had the great privilege of simply declaring Jesus in a straightforward manner, and the results were wonderful.

Many years later the apostle Paul also spoke to Jews in Jerusalem (Acts 21:17—22:22). This crowd was far more hostile than the one in Acts 2. The Jews who had not accepted Jesus by the time of Paul's speech had become hardened toward Christianity, and Paul's ministry to the Gentiles added to their resistance. But notice the similarity between Peter's message of Acts 2 and Paul's in Acts 22:2 and 3. In both cases the common ground of worldviews was already in place, and the central issue was how Jesus fit into God's plan.

The Gospel Presented to Gentiles

Do you remember Acts 1:8? What started in Jerusalem eventually spread outside Jerusalem and Judea. By the time it reached the events of Acts 10, the gospel was beginning to encounter a significant number of Gentiles. Notice, however, that those Gentiles had already been influenced by the Jewish worldview. Peter and Paul could still present the gospel of Jesus directly from the Old Testament (Acts 10; 13). But at Lystra, Paul encountered Gentiles who had no concept of the Biblical worldview. Acts 14:8-13 records what happened when Paul performed a miracle in the city of Lystra. Those people had an entirely different set of beliefs than either the Jews or the Gentiles whom Peter had encountered in Cornelius's household (Acts 10).

Paul's preaching in Lystra previewed what Paul would encounter in Athens (Acts 17:15-34). His sermon recorded in Acts 17:24-31 took into account the need for what can be called *pre-evangelism*. Paul's appeal did not begin with the direct special revelation of Scripture but with the general revelation of nature, or the created world. Paul's preaching began at the beginning. He did not start with Jesus on the cross but with God as the creator. Was Paul changing his message? Certainly not. But Paul understood that he had to build a bridge to his listeners so they could understand ideas that were foreign to them.

When Paul reached Athens, he followed his routine of speaking to the Jews and God-fearing Gentiles in the synagogue (Acts 17:17). In this setting he undoubtedly followed the teaching pattern seen in the earlier chapters of Acts. However, Paul also sought out the pagan philosophers in the marketplace (v. 17). They in turn invited him to speak in the Areopagus, or Mars Hill (see verses 17-21).

The men whom Paul addressed had worldviews that had not been shaped by the Bible. They were like the people of Lystra, not Jerusalem. When Paul began to speak, he did not begin with Scripture, but he did begin with truth.[1] The record of Paul's message (vv. 22-31) is probably a condensed form given to us by Luke, the writer of Acts (and yes, even the condensed version is still inerrant and inspired).

In his speech, Paul identified common ground that he shared with his unbelieving audience. Paul understood that they were lost, spiritually blind (2 Cor. 4:4), and spiritually dead (Eph. 2:1-3). He certainly knew that they did not have much in common with the Christian worldview. But Paul knew that all people share at least some common ground because all were created in the image of God.[2] Common ground also comes from innate knowledge that shapes the human conscience and from living in the world God created.[3] In Acts 17:22-31 Paul was applying the theology he taught in Romans 1:18-23. The response of the Athenians was mixed (Acts 17:32-34), but ultimately that response was in the hands of a sovereign God.

The Gospel Presented in the U.S.A.

What about sharing the gospel in America? Here we see a marked parallel between Athens, Georgia, of our day and Athens, Greece, of Paul's day. Gone are the days when the Christian worldview dominated America's cities and villages, its colleges, and its political institutions. America was once much like Jerusalem. The vast majority of Americans—even those who were not Christians—knew and were influenced by the Biblical or Christian worldview. The prevailing climate today is much closer to ancient Athens. We must take this fact into account when we share the gospel.

For example, no one ever thinks of Benjamin Franklin (1706–1790) as having been an evangelical Christian, because he wasn't. Franklin subscribed to a moderate form of deism. One of Franklin's best moments was his address to the Constitutional Convention that met in Philadelphia in 1787. It was one of the most critical and dangerous times in American history. Little progress was being made, and the outlook was bleak. Franklin's address emphasized the role that God actively takes in nature and in history, and Franklin requested that members of the Philadelphia clergy be invited to lead the delegates in daily prayer.

If delivered today, a speech such as Franklin's would strike many people as being out of bounds. Such open affirmation of our nation's dependence on the help and guidance of God is an uncomfortable fit with the worldviews of millions of Americans. Here is the point: Franklin wasn't even a Christian, but at least portions of the Christian worldview had deeply influenced him. He could easily converse with Christians and they with him, because the Christian worldview was so dominant in America that even non-Christians such as Franklin could speak its language.

The cultural climate is much different today. Many of our neighbors, maybe even a majority of them, have virtually no knowledge of the Bible—its truth claims, its worldview, or the specifics of the gospel. When we talk with them, we are not standing with Peter in the Jerusalem temple (Acts 3) but with Paul in the Athens Areopagus (Acts 17:19). The gospel was presented in both settings, but Athens required a different approach, and it began by Paul's first establishing some common ground.

One of the trademarks of ATW is that it suggests ways to build bridges to people who are either ignorant of the Christian worldview, hostile toward it, or both. (This bridge-building will be evident in the dialogues in part 2.) When God gives us a Jerusalem encounter, we should handle it accordingly. When in Athens, we have the example Paul left for us. In the years to come, it is reasonable to expect that more and more of our encounters with non-Christians will be on Athenian soil. Let's be ready for it.

Notes

1. The truth Paul began with was Scriptural in the sense that his proclamation reflected the Creation account found in Genesis. But Paul did not directly invoke the authority of Scripture here as he had in the Athenian synagogue (Acts 17:17). The synagogues were characterized by the study of Scripture (Acts 17:2). In the Areopagus Paul's only direct quotes were from two Greek poets (probably Epimenides and Arastus). Paul's worldview was radically different than that of the Greek poets, but where Paul found an intersection between his worldview and that of the poets, he made use of it.

2. The image of God in mankind does not refer to any physical characteristics. It speaks of certain properties of the human mind, will, and emotions. For example, mankind has the innate capacity to ponder the concept of eternality (Eccles. 3:11). Mankind has a sense of morality (Rom. 2:14 and 15). Mankind has an appreciation for beauty and is therefore motivated to create works of art. When Adam sinned and plunged humanity into sin, the image of God within mankind was deeply affected, but it was not eliminated. Even atheists bear the image of God.

3. According to Romans 2:14 and 15, God has given everyone a conscience that has some sense of right and wrong. Because of sin, the human conscience does not operate perfectly, but people are required to recognize basic morality even if they have never been exposed to God's written law.

CHAPTER 3

WHEN THEY ASK US WHY

OST unbelievers will be hard pressed to provide adequate reasons for their beliefs when we ask them why. Therefore, the ATW method provides a useful platform for proclaiming Jesus Christ. But Christians still face an important problem. What do we say when they ask *us* why?

When someone asks Christians why they believe the gospel, those believers have the duty to be ready to give a reason for their hope (1 Pet. 3:15). The purpose of this book is not to train Christians to duck these questions. Certainly we should learn to ask unbelievers tough questions about their beliefs, but not as a diversionary tactic to avoid tough questions. We will ask unbelievers questions to show them the inadequacies of their beliefs. It is against this backdrop that we can share Christ.

We All Have Faith

This chapter offers a brief lesson in how to answer tough questions. Numerous books address this issue, so the chapter will simply serve as a foundation upon which to build with additional study.[1]

Two basic truths are essential in defending the faith. First, every individual, without exception, lives by faith in something.[2] Even atheists or skeptics who dismiss faith as a crutch for the weak also live by faith—faith in themselves or in something else. Second, the faith of Christians is in God and His inspired, inerrant Word, the Bible. Upon these two truths we should build our answers.

This first truth, that every individual lives by faith in something, is the overriding focus of this book. Since any faith not rooted in the Word of God is false, it is profitable to help unbelievers see the exact content of their faith and its implications. We do this by asking a series of questions about their faith. We then explain that while we, too, live by faith, our faith is not logically self-defeating, nor does it lead to despair.[3] The people we are dealing with may still reject our faith, but they will at least have seen that their rejection is arbitrary and subjective rather than reasonable and objective. (Ultimately rejection is rooted in sin.)[4]

The Faith of Atheists

Normally we will not have difficulty getting those with a different religion to acknowledge a dependence on faith. But what about atheists who are too "wise" or too skeptical to have faith? Let's look at just a few of their beliefs held by faith.

There is no God. This statement cannot be proved. Have the atheists explored the vast universe? No. They would have to possess one of the attributes of God, omniscience, to know whether an omniscient God does not exist. *Even if atheists were right and God did not exist, they could not know it—they have to believe, or "have faith in," that idea.* Incidentally, in recent years philosophers of atheism have been, at least on the surface, moving towards agnosticism, which is easier for them to defend (Ps. 14:1; 53:1). At the same time, many scientists, such as Richard Dawkins, have become strident critics of theism and promote an openly atheistic agenda.

The universe arose by chance. This statement cannot be proved and must be held by "faith." We detect patterns and regularities that seem to belie chance occurrence and indicate design. Suppose the atheists are right and the seeming design of the universe is really just an intriguing accident; it still takes faith to hold such a view.[5] Besides, if the universe is nothing but "matter in motion," then the reasoning processes in the minds of atheists are ultimately reducible to chance occurrences, hardly a trustworthy basis for knowledge. It takes great faith to believe that human brains that result from billions of unplanned events are reliable. (This will be explained in the third encounter, "The Evolutionist," page 97.)

The sky is blue. This statement cannot be proved unless certain assumptions are in place: the basic reliability of data interpreted through the senses (sight, taste, touch, and so on). I am convinced the sky is blue, and I have better reasons for trusting sense perception than atheists do (that is a topic beyond the scope of this present book), but I am trusting sense perception, which at best is not always reliable.

Basically, it is impossible to function in this world without some type of faith. Only a being who knows all things real and potential can operate with total certainty and no faith. (Only God has such knowledge; Psalm 139:17, 18.) Do we know that a glass of orange juice will not be toxic tomorrow? No, but we assume it based on prior experience. We have enjoyed orange juice many times in the past, and it has never killed us. I surely hope that my faith in prior experiences with orange juice doesn't fail me tomorrow morning!

Why is this whole concept of faith so important? *It is because many unbelievers have not recognized just how much faith they exercise every day.* The irony is that many of these same people look askance at Christianity because of its call to live by faith (Heb. 11:6). There is much to be said for asking unbelievers pertinent questions to help them recognize their dependence upon faith.

The Faith of Religious Relativists

What about the faith commitments of those who have embraced religious relativism? These are the people who assure us that it is fine for us to believe in Jesus if that is what is true for us. Of course, all religions are fine as long as their followers are sincere and are also tolerant of other religions. This attitude is undeniably prevalent today. It is also filled with unexamined assumptions. The eighth encounter, "The Pluralist" (p. 169), addresses this issue.

The main thrust of ATW is to teach how to expose the faith commitments of conflicting worldviews and to lay them side by side with Christianity. At this point we are not simply asking unbelievers to draw an educated conclusion as to which is best. We want to show them that unless they begin with Christianity, they can't even justify the reason they are using. By the way, everyone uses reason, even those who claim to have no use for it.

The Faith of Christians

Now what about the faith of Christians? We frequently make two major errors when we discuss our faith with unbelievers. First, some Christians seem to see the admission of reliance upon faith as a potential embarrassment. Rather than openly acknowledging reliance upon Scripture as the foundation of our faith, they argue as though human reason can, completely on its own, arrive at spiritual truth—which can then be augmented by the Bible.[6] This approach gives natural man much more credit and autonomy than the Bible allows (1 Cor. 1:18–31). The other extreme is to hide behind faith as though it is superfluous to even consider possible evidences and arguments for or against the Bible. For such a Christian the unflattering stereotype of an ostrich with its head in the sand might not be far from the truth.[7]

We live by faith, and without faith it is impossible to please God (Heb. 11:6). But unlike non-Christians, we have good reasons for believing that our faith (actually the object of our faith) is reliable. It does not contain the logical contradictions inherent in other worldviews (as seen in the encounters section). Our faith provides meaningful answers to life's profound questions such as the following: Who am I? (I am a creature made in the image of God, Genesis 1:26.) Why am I here? (I am here to know God, enjoy Him, and glorify Him.) Where am I going? (Someday I will stand before God, Romans 14:12.) Why does evil exist? (Because of sin, Romans 5:12.) By faith we believe that the Word of God is exactly what it claims (2 Tim. 3:14–17). Can we absolutely prove it in such a way that non-Christians will be compelled to submit to it? No, we cannot. For unbelievers to submit to the Word of God requires more than a cogent apologetic from us, although giving one is our responsibility. It takes the work of the Holy Spirit to enable a person to believe the truth (1 Cor. 2:11, 12). Nevertheless, we have full assurance that our faith corresponds to the truth.

A Personal Note

I have considered the alternatives and find them wanting. I know what the critics have said about the Bible, and I find their objections to be rooted in philosophical bias, not fact.[8] The Bible is logically built upon its basic premise that the existence of God is a given upon which everything else is contingent (Gen. 1:1). It answers life's perplexing questions consistently and provides comfort and hope not to be found elsewhere. I am willing to base my eternal destiny on its promises. Should unbelievers continue to reject Biblical truth, that rejection is between them and God. I only ask that they be as honest about the implications of their faith as I have been with mine (see note 3). Unbelievers are free to ask me questions about my faith because I know the Bible has the answers. Some of those answers are unpopular or difficult, but they are consistent. I will ask unbelievers questions about their faith to help them see that their answers break down when those answers are scrutinized honestly.

Notes

1. A bibliography of more extensive treatments of apologetics begins on page 263. Many tough questions simply require greater familiarity with the Scriptures and the theological truths that they contain. For example, the question, What happens to innocent natives who never have an opportunity to hear about Christ? is best answered by searching Paul's letter to the Romans. At some point the answer to this question is likely to incorporate apologetics, but it primarily requires sound theology and knowledge of the Bible.

2. "Faith" can be a tricky word to define because it is multifaceted. In one sense faith is an exercise of obedience in deference to someone or something apart from oneself. This meaning seems to be the one in Romans 1:5. The object of the Christian faith is Jesus Christ, Who is the Word of God (John 1:1; Rev. 19:13). Faith in Him implies a submission to His authority and His trustworthiness, a conscious choice of assent to and belief in what He says. Faith can also be a set of beliefs or doctrine, as is found in Jude 3. (See also the definition of "faith" in Hebrews 11:1.)

3. For a justification of the centrality of logic, please see appendix E on page 249.

4. Is it even possible for unbelievers to be honest about their world-view and opposition to the gospel? In one sense the answer is no. The ravages of sin have affected mankind's thinking (Jer. 17:9; Rom. 1:18–32; 3:10–18; 1 Cor. 2:14; 2 Cor. 4:4). Opposing God is not a question of intelligence. Some of the most brilliant people in the world are opposed to Christianity. Surrendering to the truth of Christianity is a question of a moral inability or hardness. Christian apologists who minimize this dynamic are likely to adopt a method of defending the gospel that grants humans too much authority and minimizes the self-authenticating authority of the Bible. At the same time, the Bible holds each individual personally responsible for rejecting the evidence for Christianity (Acts 2:22, 23; Matt. 11:20–24). Man's spiritual blindness is not an excuse for unbelief—it is an indictment (John 10:22–39; 12:27–43). This is not a contradiction, but it does call for balance. We are not to withhold evidence or appeals to reason, but we must see them as secondary in value to the unabashed propositions in Scripture, "Thus saith the Lord God." The ATW method is one approach to apologetics/evangelism that is designed to show the folly of rejecting the authority of God's Word (see Proverbs 14:12 and 26:5), but it is not the last word in apologetics.

5. The folly of using the concept of chance as an explanation for the universe is explained in a helpful book by R. C. Sproul, *Not A Chance: The Myth of Chance in Modern Science and Cosmology* (Grand Rapids: Baker Academic, 1999).

6. It is important for the reader to understand the basic concept behind what is known as presuppositionalist apologetics. The ATW method is an attempt to employ presuppositionalism (or a modified form of it) on a practical level. I thought it best not to give a detailed definition of presuppositionalism in the main body of this book. I have provided an explanation of presuppositionalism in appendix B on page 217. The reader is strongly encouraged to read it.

7. The technical term for this position is "fideism," derived from the Latin *fides* (faith). As an extreme, fideism says that no argumentation is needed, permitted, or will be offered. Fideism says, "I believe because I believe" and tells others that they should not do anything more than "just believe it because it is true."

There are numerous evidences for the reliability of the Bible and the resurrection of Jesus Christ. The wonder of the Incarnation is that God entered human history in bodily form. We can see Christ's footprints in the history record. I believe that some presuppositionalist apologists mistakenly minimize the utility of historical evidences and the Biblical approval of using evidences.

8. It is helpful for believers to know something about the attacks against the Bible and the many profitable rebuttals prepared by Christian apologists. Many books that defend the integrity of the Bible are readily available for the interested reader. One work I have found particularly helpful is *Historical Criticism of the Bible: Methodology or Ideology?* by Eta Linnemann (Grand Rapids: Kregel Publications, 2001). Newer books are constantly being published that address the same issues that Linnemann addresses in her book.

CHAPTER 4

THE "BLESSING" OF IMMORALITY

I S THERE any good news? A quick review of any major newspaper or evening news show on TV reveals that immorality is a growing but unchecked menace. Murder rates soar and locked doors don't always protect the innocent. Several school buildings have become battlefields with multiple murders. Political leaders promise change and deliver more of the same old corruption. Traditional Christian values are trampled underfoot. Teen suicide is all too common. Millions of marriages end in bitterness. Babies are destroyed while in their mothers' wombs, but the destruction is declared a good thing because a woman should be able to do what she wants with her body. The entertainment industry provides increasingly degenerate fare, and people still want more. Religious denominations that once declared God's Word and stood for something now have their pulpits filled by avowed skeptics and those who call evil good (Isa. 5:20). Good news to encourage Christians is quite scarce.

However, Christians might, in one sense, find that the rampant apostasy and immorality of our day could be a source of blessing. In fact, the current plague of immorality might be one of the best developments for the cause of Christ in many years. How? Can Christians legitimately be glad for immorality? After all, immorality is an affront to our holy God. Nevertheless, it also provides Christians with an opportunity to effectively proclaim the superiority of the Biblical worldview.[1] As we proclaim the Biblical worldview, we declare the gospel and invite people to believe it (Acts 16:31).

God Meant It for Good

Consider the important Biblical precedent found in the life of Joseph. The account of Joseph's life in Genesis 37—50 clearly shows that Joseph was the victim of immorality practiced by his brothers. Not only did they sell Joseph into slavery; they provided their father, Jacob, with deceptive evidence that Joseph had been killed.

In the years that followed, Joseph was also victimized by the immorality of Potiphar's wife (Gen. 39). Yet God was faithful, and eventually Joseph rose to a place of prominence in Egypt. When Joseph's brothers came to Egypt years later seeking relief from a destructive famine, they crossed paths with Joseph. When Joseph revealed his true identity to them, they were fearful, which is not surprising; they had tried to ruin his life because of their jealousy. Joseph's words to his brothers instruct us regarding the upside of immorality. Joseph explained to them that what they had meant for evil, God had intended to use for good (Gen. 50:20). In other words, while we might not relish the increase of immorality, it is legitimate for the Christian to expect God to use it to accomplish His purposes. (See also Ephesians 1:11 and Isaiah 10:5-27.) We can use this Biblical truth in our attempt to proclaim the gospel.

We should not underestimate the prevalence of this principle in the Scriptures. Perhaps the most significant example is the arrest, trial, and crucifixion of Jesus. The wickedness of those who participated in Christ's death is undeniable. Motivated by jealousy, hatred, greed, pride, power, and self-righteousness, the conspirators murdered not only an innocent man but the very Son of God. But what about God's working through those circumstances? In his sermon to the Jews at Pentecost, Peter stated that the events that led to Jesus' death, including the crucifixion itself, were part of God's plan to provide redemption for sinful men (Acts 2:23; 4:27, 28). Certainly God will justly deal with the sinful actions of the conspirators. Just because their actions contributed to our redemption, we in no way seek to excuse those actions. What we are endeavoring to do is recognize the Biblical teaching that God can bring good out of the evil deeds of sinful men. Just as Israel learned at the Red Sea, we know that God can use the pharaohs of our day to bring glory to Himself and victory to His people (Exod. 14:17, 18).

God Has Given Man a Conscience

The second principle that reveals that immorality is an opportunity for apologetics and evangelism is the important truth that all men have a God-given conscience. In Romans 2:14 and 15 Paul taught his friends in Rome that even the Gentiles who did not have the written Word of God with its moral precepts still had an innate sense of right and wrong that had been placed in their hearts by the Creator. Some people have sinned so grievously and so long that they have managed to sear, or numb, their consciences (1 Tim. 4:2). Nevertheless, most people around the world share several common moral beliefs.

Informed Christians can appeal to the God-given conscience within unbelievers.[2] Only the Christian worldview can harmonize the existence of the conscience with the world in which we live. Unbelievers may rely on their consciences, but without a

Biblical framework they have no way of justifying that reliance. Once we Christians understand this fact, we can use it with great effectiveness. A fundamental premise of this book is that unbelievers have innate moral standards but cannot truly account for them outside Christianity.[3] The ATW method is designed to expose this fact.

To help understand how the conscience works, Christians might profit from reading *Mere Christianity* by the great British author C. S. Lewis. Writing shortly after the conclusion of World War II, Lewis elaborated on Romans 2:14 and 15 with this classic argument:

> This law was called the Law of Nature because people thought that every one knew it by nature and did not need to be taught it. They did not mean, of course, that you might not find an odd individual here and there who did not know it, just as you find a few people who are color-blind or have no ear for a tune. But taking the race as a whole, they thought that the human idea of decent behavior was obvious to every one. And I believe they were right. If they were not, then all the things we said about the war were nonsense. What was the sense in saying the enemy were in the wrong unless Right is a real thing which the Nazis at bottom knew as well as we did and ought to have practiced? If they had had no notion of what we mean by right, then, though we might still have had to fight them, we could no more have blamed them for that than for the color of their hair.[4]

What Lewis wrote is borne out daily in human experience. His writings are an amplification of the principle Paul stated in Romans 2:14 and 15: "For when Gentiles, who do not have the law, by nature do the things in the law, these, although not having the law, are a law to themselves, who show the work of the law written in their hearts, their conscience also bearing witness, and between themselves their thoughts accusing or else excusing them."

How can this common sense of right and wrong aid the Christian in evangelism? The answer is that the rampant immorality of our day bothers more people than just Christians. As our culture reels under the weight of moral decay, more and more people are demanding something be done. Consequently, many politicians see the advantage of portraying themselves as being committed to solid moral values. Certainly this appeal is directed to a larger audience than just Christians. When all is said and done, however, only Christians can truly provide a logical basis for the morality that so many non-Christians want to see return to our country. Even unbelievers who aren't concerned about their own immorality still care when they are affected by the immorality of others.

Lewis was correct when he observed that people often reject moral precepts in their own lives but still want others to live by them. We are familiar with the chronic cry of protest sent our way when we confront people with God's moral absolutes. People naturally want to indulge their flesh. Usually they have some degree of appreciation for how unattractive the world would be if all people felt free to do whatever they wanted (and a frightening number of people are doing exactly that). Several Christian ethicists have pointed out that a person's true ethical values are not to be found in how he treats others, but in how he expects to be treated.

God Is Still on the Throne

Yes, it is distressing to see what is happening in our society. Murder, rape, corruption, domestic violence, sexual anarchy, divorce, chemical abuse, suicide—all seem more prevalent with each passing year. But praise God! He is still on the throne, and He can use faithful Christians to accomplish good and glorious

things in spite of men's evil hearts and intentions. The God
Whom we serve has written eternity on the hearts of all men
(Eccles. 3:11) and has given His creatures a conscience with
which they must contend. We Christians alone have the answers
that truly solve the dilemma of man's conscience. When we encounter unbelievers who think their way is better than God's
way, we will ask them why. In several of the encounters portrayed in the second part of this book, the Christian will ask questions designed to speak to the non-Christian's sense of right and
wrong. The inevitable flaws in the unbeliever's answers will serve
to remind us that this is indeed an exciting and opportune time
to be alive and to share the gospel.

It is important that Christians understand the nature of this
argument. Someone once pointed out that consequences do not
refute; they explain. The fact that non-Christian worldviews
break down or that Christianity provides a cogent system of ethics does not, in and of itself, prove Christianity. If we argue in
that manner, we are simply being pragmatic (i.e., "our system
works best so it is the one that should be used").

We are not trying to persuade unbelievers of something that
is new to them or was not previously known. Our challenge is
not merely that they compare all the competing systems of ethics
with the hope that they will conclude that the preponderance of
evidence points to Christianity (even though it does). The Bible
declares that sinners already know the righteous moral requirements of a holy God (Rom. 2:14–16) and suppress that truth
(Rom. 1:18–32). Read the text carefully. "The wrath of God
is revealed . . . against all ungodliness and unrighteousness of
men, who suppress the truth. . . . What may be known of God is
manifest in them. . . . They are without excuse. . . . Although
they knew God, they did not glorify Him as God, nor were
thankful. . . . They did not like to retain God in their knowledge"
(vv. 18–28).

There is a sense in which the theology of Romans 1 and 2 indicates that our primary communication with unbelievers should be one of proclamation. After all, they already have some innate knowledge of God, and they are suppressing it. They don't need evidence and argument as much as they need to be confronted with the gospel and called to repentance.

We Proclaim the Gospel and Expose False Thinking

Of course, our goal will always be the proclamation of the gospel. However, the Bible allows for different ways of framing the gospel message, especially when our message meets opposition. Interacting with man's innate moral awareness (which includes his expectations of how others should treat him) in the midst of contemporary ethical confusion is a legitimate context for the gospel message. The writer of Proverbs stated, "There is a way that seems right to a man, but its end is the way of death" (14:12). If unbelievers reject the gospel that we proclaim to them, they should be asked questions that expose the inevitable outcome of choosing a way that seems right to man.

We are not simply suggesting that the evidence points to Christianity. We are unequivocally stating that it is true by the authority of God's Word. It is to be presupposed from the start (see appendix B, page 217). If people balk at this authority (and unless the Holy Spirit intervenes, they will), then we will show them where that folly leads. (See the explanation of Proverbs 14:12 and Proverbs 26:4 and 5 in chapter 6.) The ATW method is designed to do this. The blight of immorality gives us a tremendous opportunity for applying ATW. To paraphrase Joseph, "What sinful man intends for evil, God intends for good!"

Notes

1. Many of the encounters in this book deal with the inability of non-Christian worldviews to provide a reliable system of ethics. Technically, this approach to apologetics is known as the moral argument for God. I am convinced that this is a rich mine barely tapped by the Christian community. This line of argumentation is consistent with presuppositionalism, but it is just as frequently employed by evidentialists. C. S. Lewis's *The Abolition of Man* is one of many valuable presentations available to Christian readers. Please see appendix F (p. 253) for background on the formal study of ethics.

2. A small minority of commentators contend that Romans 2:14 and 15 refer to believing Gentiles who participate in the New Covenant. I do not think the context of Romans 1—3 supports that view. The interpretation of Romans 2:14 and 15 as used in *Ask Them Why* stands in the mainstream of conservative scholarship.

3. Paul was not saying that human beings innately know the story of Christ's redemptive work. That knowledge requires what is called special revelation and is learned through Scripture. Mankind's innate or immediate knowledge, which is placed in men and women by God, includes but is not necessarily limited to an awareness of God as Creator, God as a holy being (thus moral standards), and God as a righteous judge (thus mankind's accountability). Perhaps it can be stated like this: The innate knowledge of God that humans have is enough to leave them condemned and without excuse. The knowledge they need to be saved depends on Christians' sharing the gospel message.

4. C. S. Lewis, *Mere Christianity* (New York: The Macmillan Co., 1952), 18, 19.

CHAPTER 5

THE PROBLEM
OF EVIL

I N OUR efforts to use the blight of immorality to promote
the superiority of the Biblical worldview, we also need to
be prepared to answer those who use the existence of immorality and evil to attack the Bible. In other words, the
very thing that this book contends is an asset to evangelism has
frequently been used as a weapon in attacking the Biblical worldview.

Used to Discredit the Idea of God

The problem of evil and its alleged refutation of Christianity
have been presented in many forms, but the basic approach is
the one proposed by the philosopher Epicurus more than two
thousand years ago. Epicurus's argument was as follows: The
existence of evil negates the possibility of an omnipotent, omniscient, benevolent God. If God wants to destroy evil but cannot,
He is not omnipotent. If He can destroy evil but does not want to,

He is not benevolent. If He wants to destroy evil and has the power to destroy it but does not have the necessary knowledge, He is not omniscient. The continued existence of evil makes it logically impossible to accept the existence of an omnipotent, omniscient, benevolent God.

This is the very argument used by atheist Frank Zindler in a debate with Christian apologist Dr. William Lane Craig held on June 27, 1993, and attended by several thousand people and broadcast live on numerous Christian radio stations around the country. The debate was designed to assess the evidence for or against the existence of God. Zindler used the argument of Epicurus exactly as we've just noted to discredit the idea of God.

Many people have the same view as Epicurus and Zindler, even though they may not have articulated it as precisely. We all know people who have doubted either God's goodness, His power, or His existence during the pain of seeing a loved one struggle with cancer, "unanswered" prayers for an unfaithful spouse preparing to abandon a family, the sexual abuse of a small child, the death of thousands in an earthquake, and other traumas that occur in this world. Christians themselves have also been susceptible to doubting God over painful things that have happened to them. If Christians struggle in this area, it is certainly easy to see why non-Christians at least temporarily doubt the God of the Bible.

Affects Evangelism

Feelings about this subject can be quite strong. Many people have been victims of natural or moral evil and cannot help but wonder how the God Whom they have heard about can allow such things to happen. There is a sound theological argument that explains these things, but the vast majority of unbelievers are unaware of it. Unfortunately, many Christians cannot articulate a reasonable theodicy. The minority of Christians who are well grounded theologically still must wrestle with the reality of these traumas that can test the faith of even the strongest Christian. Christians must be ready to deal with this issue in evangelism.

One incident that stands out in my mind taught me an important lesson on the problem of evil and its impact on evangelism. As a freshman at a Bible college, I was involved in weekly street-witnessing efforts in the city of Scranton, Pennsylvania. A program in the downtown area provided office space for people to walk in, sit down, and talk about their problems. I liked to go there because I was always likely to find at least one person seeking to talk about life's issues. One night I took my roommate with me, and we walked into a room where a few people were seated and casually talking. I was soon engaged in the most one-sided conversation ever!

The conversation began when I approached a man who appeared to be in his mid-forties and who was a little rough around the edges. I greeted him with a friendly hello. Before I could say one additional word, he ripped into me with a rather loud string of obscenities. He had correctly identified me as a Bible college student, and he had no intention of letting me say one word about Christ. After he finished cursing me, he started attacking God's character. He was upset that just a few nights earlier a tragic fire had taken the life of a two-year-old child. Not really looking for an answer but trying to vent his hostility, he asked me how God could possibly permit such a thing to happen.

There was not much I could say; he had really caught me off guard. Looking back at that incident, I am not sure if a civil conversation would have been possible. Perhaps the man was truly disturbed by the problem of evil, or his question may simply have been an attempt to avoid hearing the gospel. Whatever his motivation, I saw firsthand the challenge that the problem of evil poses to Christians who want to share their faith.

Used to Establish the Biblical Worldview

Has the Biblical worldview met an insurmountable obstacle? Are we hurting our case by citing immorality and evil to employ the ATW approach? Would we be better served by trying to avoid the issue altogether?

A thorough treatment of the problem of evil is outside the scope of this book.[1] Nevertheless a few key points can be made to verify the usefulness of evil in establishing the Biblical worldview using the ATW method.

Regarding Epicurus's line of thought, it is now commonly acknowledged an inadequate argument due to missing premises. In other words, the argument fails to take into account several possible factors that would affect the argument. Consider these three factors.

First, God might have good reasons for delaying the ending of evil. This perspective is indicated in 2 Peter 3:9 and 10, which point out that God will end evil and that non-Christians are fortunate He has not yet done so.

Second, evil can be useful in producing good (see Genesis 50:20).

Third, perhaps it would be a greater evil for evil not to exist because it would prevent man from being morally free. (I don't necessarily accept this premise, but the skeptic cannot just ignore it.)

Another consideration is the inconsistency of atheists like the aforementioned Mr. Zindler in using standards of good and evil. The problem of evil cannot even be legitimately raised by atheists. If there is no God, then "good" and "evil" are terms lacking any ultimate meaning, and it is therefore invalid to use evil to castigate Christianity. I once debated a philosophy student on the campus of a state university.[2] He raised the problem of evil and passionately described the death of his grandmother due to bone cancer. He argued that if a good God existed, such things would not happen. As the debate progressed, I led him to admit that, according to atheism, human beings have no intrinsic value and that they are the products of "matter in motion." Gently but firmly, I showed him that since he believed this, his grandmother was nothing but a "biological bag of stuff" with no intrinsic value, so her death was just a value-neutral process of an uncaused universe. He was being completely inconsistent in his complaint against the evil of cancer. I then shared with him that the wonderful thing about Christianity is that his grandmother truly did matter as a person. (This concept will be developed in the encounters section of this book.)

The problem of evil has always been an issue that provokes conflict, both emotional and rational. Nevertheless, Christianity has the answers to this problem. When dealing with unbelievers who reject the Biblical view of evil in favor of something else, ask them why.

Notes

1. For a clear, effective treatment of the issue of evil, I highly recommend *Faith and Reason: Searching for a Rational Faith* by Ronald Nash (Grand Rapids: Zondervan, 1988). His explanation is useful to any Christian who is serious about asking and answering questions when dealing with unbelievers. John Frame also provides a helpful treatment of the problem in *Apologetics to the Glory of God: An Introduction* (Phillipsburg, NJ: Presbyterian and Reformed Publishing Co., 1994). Christian apologists have different ways of handling this issue. As finite creatures who trust God, we must not be afraid to appeal to Deuteronomy 29:29 when dealing with unbelievers. Their worldview is hopelessly inadequate on this issue. We are not out of line when, from time to time, we simply portray unbelievers for what they are: rebels who fail to submit to God's Word, not because it is inadequate but because they do not want to submit.

2. The opening presentation that I used in this debate can be found in appendix C, page 225.

CHAPTER 6

THE BIBLICAL FOUNDATION

THE encounters in part 2 are intended to provide examples of how Christians can share Christ with unbelievers. The encounters do not include a full presentation of the gospel, as important as that is. The intention of the Christian to present the gospel is assumed in each dialogue. The encounters are primarily designed to show the errors of unbelief in keeping with the following Biblical considerations.

Americans Live in "Athens"

"Now while Paul waited for them at Athens, his spirit was provoked within him when he saw that the city was given over to idols. Therefore he reasoned in the synagogue with the Jews and with the Gentile worshipers, and in the marketplace daily with those who happened to be there" (Acts 17:16, 17).

As explained in chapter 2, Christians living in America to-day are not living in Jerusalem but in Athens. This fact has many implications for apologetics. The Jerusalem-Athens comparison reflects the prevailing intellectual and spiritual climate in our culture. In the book of Acts, the early Christians began their ministry in the city of Jerusalem. Although the city was not Christian, the people were willing to take the Scriptures (the Hebrew Old Testament) seriously. They already acknowledged the existence of Jehovah, the possibility of miracles, and the promise of Messiah. But as Christianity began to spread, it eventually encountered cultures with far less common ground. Acts 17:16–34 records Paul's visit to Athens. In Athens the existence of Jehovah was not acknowledged, the Hebrew Scriptures were not well-known, and the possibility of a physical resurrection was almost incomprehensible. (Many schools of Greek philosophy taught that the body is a prison and that death brings release. To speak of being resurrected into a glorified physical body was foolishness to Greeks.)

In his approach to the Athenians, Paul had to lay some groundwork that would not have been necessary in Jerusalem. This groundwork is what we mean by the term "pre-evangelism."

There was a time when American culture was more like Jerusalem than Athens. Even among non-Christians it was rare to find hard-boiled secularism and total disregard for and ignorance of the Scriptures. Today America is more like Athens. Christians need to adjust their approach accordingly (while the message remains unchanged). ATW is designed to be a tool for pre-evangelism in America's version of Athens.

We Are Commanded to "Do" Apologetics

"But sanctify the Lord God in your hearts, and always be ready to give a defense to everyone who asks you a reason for the hope that is in you, with meekness and fear" (1 Pet. 3:15).

This verse is perhaps the most famous of verses used in the study of apologetics. When Peter said that believers must be ready always to give an answer, he used the Greek word *apologia,* from which comes our term "apologetics." Besides his command that we be ready, Peter added two other requirements. First, we Christians are to honor Christ as Lord of our lives, and this command includes the way we think. In other words, we don't tell unbelievers that we will temporarily set aside our commitment to the Bible and reason with them on neutral ground. Unbelievers are rebels (just as we were before God graciously saved us), and they are definitely not neutral. In responding to Peter's command to honor the lordship of Jesus Christ, John Frame explained,

> Some theologians present apologetics as if it were almost an exception to this commitment. They tell us that when we argue with unbelievers, we should not argue based on criteria or standards derived from the Bible. To argue that way, they say, would be biased. We should rather present to the unbeliever an unbiased argument, one that makes no religious assumptions pro or con, one that is neutral. We should, on this view, use criteria and standards that the unbeliever himself can accept. So logic, facts, experience, reason, and such become the sources of truth. Divine revelation, especially Scripture, is systematically excluded.[1]

Although it is appropriate to deal with the unbeliever by using logic, facts, experience, and reason, we must always insist that only by acknowledging God can these things be justified.

Second, it is important that Christians display humility and gentleness when dealing with unbelievers. Prepared Christians can dismantle the arguments of most unbelievers, but this ability should in no way make them proud. It is by grace alone that anyone has been saved so that no man can boast. Since we have

Human Beings Know That God Exists

"For the wrath of God is revealed from heaven against all ungodliness and unrighteousness of men, who suppress the truth in unrighteousness, because what may be known of God is manifest in them, for God has shown it to them. For since the creation of the world His invisible attributes are clearly seen, being understood by the things that are made, even His eternal power and Godhead, so that they are without excuse" (Rom. 1:18–20).

In their hearts, men know that God exists because this is how God has created them. Even though men might go so far as to deny the existence of God (Paul called this act "suppressing the truth"), they live as though there is a God. Men appeal to moral absolutes even as they deny their existence; they appeal to logic even though a godless universe cannot adequately account for the existence of logic. They believe in an orderly universe that permits science even though a universe lacking design, arising by chance, and doomed to extinction makes the conditions needed for science impossible. Every time men try to use reason seriously, they are showing their dependence upon the very God they are quick to deny; therefore, they have no excuse for their unbelief. The great Christian apologist Cornelius Van Til pointed out that non-Christians are living on "borrowed capital." What Van Til meant by this description is that unbelievers live as though they think the world makes sense. But to have this view they must borrow from the very worldview they seek to deny. This is the ultimate act of self-deception, or suppressing the truth.

The truth in Romans 1:18–20 should add to our confidence

when we deal with unbelievers. In a sense we know unbelievers better than they know themselves. We recognize what they are doing (suppressing the truth about God) even if they do not. We should not be afraid of being blunt about this fact. (Love and bluntness do not necessarily contradict each other.)

This passage does not merely speak of the thought processes of atheists and agnostics. Romans 1:25 says that unbelievers have exchanged the truth for a lie, an act often cloaked in religious activity.

Humans Possess Innate Knowledge of Morality

"For when Gentiles, who do not have the law, by nature do the things in the law, these, although not having the law, are a law to themselves, who show the work of the law written in their hearts, their conscience also bearing witness, and between themselves their thoughts accusing or else excusing them" (Rom. 2:14, 15).

This passage is the absolute heart and soul of ATW. Paul taught that man possesses innate knowledge in the realm of morality given to him by God. In the immediate context of Paul's epistle to the Romans, Paul was in the process of establishing his argument that all of mankind is both morally aware of God and accountable to God. "All mankind" includes Jews who have the law of God in written form (the law of Moses) and Gentiles who have the law of God written on their hearts (the internal conscience). Jews and Gentiles alike are guilty of violating God's law and thus fall short of the glory of God (Rom. 3:23). Incidentally, this fact eliminates the question, What happens to the innocent who never hear the gospel? Whatever ignorant men are, they are not innocent.

C. S. Lewis's argument from *Mere Christianity* has already been cited (p. 46). For all his sinfulness and rejection of moral absolutes, man just cannot seem to shake his belief in right and wrong. Moral relativists are no exception, despite their outward protestations to the contrary. This process will be seen in the encounters that are to follow. I have heard many atheists, moral relativists, and secular humanists debate and lecture, and I have yet to find one who truly and consistently lives in a manner that refutes Romans 2:14 and 15. Christians should always be ready to lovingly challenge unbelievers to deal with the conscience God has given them.

In making use of Romans 2:14 and 15 we are not claiming that the human conscience works perfectly. Far from it. Man's sinfulness greatly hinders the spirit with which he thinks. But this passage teaches that God Himself is the source of the human conscience, and so it becomes a valuable point of contact between Christians and non-Christians.

Non-Christian Worldviews Fail

"There is a way that seems right to a man, but its end is the way of death" (Prov. 14:12).

Since Adam and Eve first chose to reject God's Word and follow their own way, an endless stream of evidence has shown that all systems that rebel against God are tragically mistaken. When man uses his own criteria for determining essential issues of life—such as ultimate meaning, purpose, and value systems—and refuses to submit to the Word of God, the seeds of his eventual destruction are planted. Christians can often demonstrate this Biblical truth by taking a non-Christian worldview and carrying it to its logical conclusion. This process will be demonstrated in the encounters.

We Must Not Reason on Non-Christian Terms

"Do not answer a fool according to his folly, lest you also be like him. Answer a fool according to his folly, lest he be wise in his own eyes" (Prov. 26:4, 5).

At first glance these two verses seem to contradict each other, but actually they are complimentary. When dealing with individuals who have rejected God's Word, we must not lower ourselves to their level by reasoning apart from the Word. To do so would be granting validity to their sinful exercise of autonomy. There is a sense, however, in which it is helpful to grant them their autonomy solely for the purpose of showing them the folly of their unbelief. We don't grant that their autonomy is valid, but we use it to turn it against itself and point out its devastating consequences.

Moral Relativism Fails

"In those days there was no king in Israel; everyone did what was right in his own eyes" (Judg. 21:25).

A reading of the book of Judges leaves one amazed at the decadence and turmoil of a nation that had been founded upon the law of Moses. Yet the debilitating condition of Israel was the logical consequence of its rejection of God's absolutes and its replacing them with human relativism. The disastrous outcome was predictable both by experience and logic.

The material found in Judges 17—21 is especially disturbing (see 17:6 and 19:1). The lack of a king was not the root problem. The proper role of the king, had Israel possessed one, would have been to mediate God's authority to men. At that point in history, the last thing the people wanted was to genuinely submit to God's authority. Technically speaking, Israel had a King, and His name was Jehovah (1 Sam. 8:6-9). The people rejected Jehovah's authority, and the results were the events of Judges 17—21. Proverbs 14:12 is directly related to this truth. In several of the encounters in part 2, Christians will force unbelievers to see where moral relativism leads. As you study the encounters, keep Judges 21:25 in mind. I believe this approach provides one of the clearest arguments available for the Biblical worldview.

We Seek to Identify Flaws in Human Thinking

"For it is written: 'I will destroy the wisdom of the wise, and bring to nothing the understanding of the prudent.' Where is the wise? Where is the scribe? Where is the disputer of this age? Has not God made foolish the wisdom of this world?" (1 Cor. 1:19, 20).

As the creator and ruler of the universe, God has permitted man to use his mind to develop philosophies that deny Him. However, no matter how clever and complex a philosophy may be, man cannot devise a philosophy that can stand when honestly compared to God's Word. Since God has made foolish the wisdom of this world, Christians should seek to identify the flaws in unbelievers' systems of thought. Certainly rejection of God by human thinking is wrong, but Paul seemed to indicate something more; that is, any unbiblical system is demonstrably foolish once its logical vulnerability is exposed.

Do not interpret this admonition as an appeal to spend thousands of hours studying other systems of belief or thought. Christians should primarily master Biblical theology. There are too many false systems in the world for any one Christian to master them all. Our time here on earth is too short and precious, unless God has specifically called a believer to specialize in such studies. I believe that Christians who really understand the unique nature of Christianity can handle any non-Christian system even if they don't know a lot about it.

We Must Not Ignore the Sinful Pretensions of Man

"For though we walk in the flesh, we do not war according to the flesh. For the weapons of our warfare are not carnal but mighty in God for pulling down strongholds, casting down arguments and every high thing that exalts itself against the knowledge of God" (2 Cor. 10:3-5).

Sinful man has built several worldviews that stand in opposition to the truths revealed in Scripture. This is an act of pride and is very much an insult to God. Christians must not be content to ignore these sinful pretensions. Of 2 Corinthians 10:3-5 Richard Pratt stated:

> As those who love God and His Word, believers in Christ are to be "destroying speculations and every lofty thing raised up against the knowledge of God." Unbelievers try with great persistence to replace the knowledge of God with some other notion. Since Christians are aware of the importance of acknowledging God in all areas of life, they should be committed to challenging and destroying those substitutes. Loving God compels us to attack all idols produced by men.[2]

To Pratt's astute comments we would add that a genuine and compassionate burden for the souls of lost men and women will also compel us to tear down these idolatrous substitutes.

We Must Not Reject Reason

"But he said, 'I am not mad, most noble Festus, but speak the words of truth and reason'" (Acts 26:25).

Rejection of God's Word is not an exercise in truth and reason, but the rejection of them. Paul's presentation to Agrippa and Festus could have been rejected (and apparently was) but not because Paul was guilty of an irrational approach that appealed to blind faith. It takes faith to believe unto salvation (Heb. 11:6), but it takes a greater amount of faith to reject God's Word yet be convinced one's alternative worldview is valid. Christians should not see reason as an independent entity that is the key to converting non-Christians. The ability to use reason is due to our being created in the image of God. Rejecting the use of reason is every bit as unbiblical as granting to reason autonomy apart from God's Word. Reason, *used in submission to revelation,* was Paul's methodology, and it should be ours as well. Christians should not criticize unbelievers for using reason, but for using reason without acknowledging the Creator Who makes reason possible. Paul reasoned with unbelievers, but he did so without denying the ultimate authority, the Word of God. It is wrong to deprecate reason, for our ability to reason is a gift from God. It is just as wrong to elevate human reason to the place where it sits in judgment over God's Word.

We Don't Convert People; The Holy Spirit Does

"For the word of God is living and powerful, and sharper than any two-edged sword, piercing even to the division of soul and spirit, and of joints and marrow, and is a discerner of the thoughts and intents of the heart" (Heb. 4:12).

I have saved this verse for near the end because I want it to serve as a reminder that the ultimate power of conversion is not to be found in our ability to do apologetics. I love apologetics, and I believe in apologetics, but the Word of God has a supernatural authority and power that can change even the hardest of hearts. As you read the encounters in part 2, you will see that the emphasis is on the apologetical method of ATW. Please note that each encounter can lend itself to a proclamation of Biblical truth at any point. Remember, you can share your faith even if you are not trained in apologetics. It is because of our desire to be as effective as possible that we study apologetics.

Evangelism and Apologetics Require Compassion

"Then Jesus went about all the cities and villages, teaching in their synagogues, preaching the gospel of the kingdom, and healing every sickness and every disease among the people. But when He saw the multitudes, He was moved with compassion for them,

because they were weary and scattered, like sheep having no shepherd. Then He said to His disciples, 'The harvest truly is plentiful, but the laborers are few. Therefore pray the Lord of the harvest to send out laborers into His harvest'" (Matt. 9:35-38).

Compassion for the lost is a prerequisite for using the ATW method. We must never lose sight of the importance of human souls, even of those who have rejected the truth.

Biblical compassion leads to action. Many more passages in the Bible touch upon evangelism and apologetics. The twelve passages cited here were chosen because of their helpfulness in explaining the ATW method. The Word of God is true and it is powerful (Heb. 4:12). May God grant His people the passion and the spirit of obedience to put it into practice.

Notes

1. John Frame, *Apologetics to the Glory of God: An Introduction* (Phillipsburg, NJ: Presbyterian and Reformed Publishing Co., 1994), 4.

2. Richard Pratt, Jr., *Every Thought Captive* (Phillipsburg, NJ: Presbyterian and Reformed Publishing Co., 1979), ix.

Part 2

ASK THEM WHY

ENCOUNTERS

INTRODUCTION

PRESUPPOSITIONS, WORLDVIEWS, AND ATW

THE following encounters are designed to show how an awareness of the verses discussed in chapter 6 and others like them can provide a reliable basis for the ATW approach to evangelism. In each of the encounters, the Christian is going to ask questions for the purpose of uncovering the basic assumptions or presuppositions upon which the unbeliever has built his or her worldview. As important as presuppositions are, it is amazing how seldom they are evaluated. All people have presuppositions, and thinking cannot take place without them. What is a presupposition? A presupposition is a primary or foundational belief through which all other information is interpreted.

Here is an example of a presupposition in action. I am sitting in a chair in my office. Do I believe this chair exists? This question might seem ridiculous, but how do I even know that this chair exists? How would most people establish the existence of the chair? Most people will answer the question by appealing to sense perception. By this they mean that since they can see the chair with their own eyes, it surely exists. Not only that, they can touch the chair and feel that it exists. When the chair swivels, it squeaks, and they can hear it.

Is this a valid way to test for the existence of the chair? For the most part it is, but such an approach is employing a presupposition, a vitally important one that usually goes unexamined. What is this presupposition? It is the belief that information gathered through the senses (in this case sight, touch, and hearing) is reliable and corresponds to reality. All that we learn through our senses we consider to be true because we are operating on a belief that presupposes this concept.

There is a big problem with building a worldview upon this presupposition. What is it? The problem is that many people see, feel, and hear things that do not exist! I have had the sad experience of dealing with people who, due to mental illness or substance abuse, were seeing things, feeling things, or hearing things that were not real. Yet to such people the sensations were so vivid that I could not persuade them that the sensations were not real. We live our lives accepting as a presupposition that our senses are basically reliable, yet we are sharing the world with people who seemingly disprove the assumption.

How is this dilemma resolved? Again, most people would probably say something to the effect that delusions are highly individualistic. If I brought one hundred people into my office to see, touch, and hear the chair, and all one hundred people confirmed my observations, then that would be conclusive proof that my senses are reliable. But would it be? How do I know that the one hundred people I invite to examine my chair even exist? Is it not possible that I am actually in a psychiatric ward and I am imagining the chair plus the one hundred people?

Is there an escape to this problem? Is there some way to know that the presuppositions I choose are sound? Must I surrender the belief that my chair exists? If you have never thought like this before, then perhaps you are starting to see how important presuppositions are. Presuppositions are central when dealing with unbelievers. Their beliefs reflect their presuppositions because their beliefs grow out of their presuppositions.

In the following encounters, the Christians will ask the non-Christians questions designed to reveal the latter's assumptions or presuppositions. Worldviews built on unbiblical presuppositions cannot stand the test of reason and internal consistency. (See appendix C, page 225, for an explanation of this claim.) Unbelief can be reduced to absurdity even though people continue to practice it. What then does all this questioning accomplish? It *questioning* demonstrates that human thought that is opposed to the Bible is self-defeating and that only by submitting to the Word of God can one find a consistent basis for a true philosophy of life. When the Christian questions the unbeliever in a genuine spirit of love and humility, it brings glory to God.

Until a person is willing to give up his allegiance to his own primacy and submit to God, he cannot be saved. It goes without saying that many people have accepted the gospel of Jesus Christ without being conscious of a change in presuppositions, but such a change has occurred. Only God in His sovereignty can bring about such a change of heart and mind, but as His servants we should focus our efforts on proclaiming the gospel in a context that is sensitive to presuppositions.

This sort of pre-evangelism can be useful in building a bridge[1] to an unbeliever so that we can share the gospel message of the redemptive work of Christ. However, there is much more to the Christian worldview than just the atoning work of Christ. The Christian worldview provides a foundation for ethics, logic,[2] science, and every sphere of human activity. One of the major weaknesses of the contemporary church is that it has largely failed to engage the world in all these spheres of life. Consequently, it is common to find people (even Christians) who believe that faith is strictly a private matter to be kept in the home or at church gatherings. It is not surprising that entire segments of society (educators, government officials, scientists, and so forth) see matters of faith as being irrelevant in their specialized domains.

Besides being dangerously misguided, this attitude further marginalizes the gospel message. The encounters you are about to read show Christians who are ready and willing to share the gospel, but their approach to unbelievers casts a wider net than simply quoting John 3:16 or distributing gospel tracts, as essential as that is.

If an unbeliever is open to the gospel at the beginning of a conversation, we can skip the pre-evangelism. The person's openness might evidence that the Holy Spirit is already at work in his heart. The ATW method is for times when we encounter unbelievers who attempt to hide behind intellectual walls of unbelief.

Notes

1. I have tried to use dialogue in the encounters that will demonstrate a logical progression toward a gospel presentation. The grammar and sentence structure in the conversations have an inevitable artificiality. In a normal conversation between two people, the spoken word is expressed somewhat differently than the written word. My hope is that the reader will look past this weakness and focus on the nature of the ATW method being portrayed.

2. Once again, the reader is encouraged to read appendix E, page 249, for an explanation of the role of logic.

THE PRAGMATIST

UNBELIEVER: Phil, a thirty-one-year-old businessman with ambition. He desires to climb the corporate ladder. He has begun to work in the same corporation as Daniel, and the two men have gotten to know each other. They have a friendly relationship with each other, but Phil politely refuses to consider the spiritual principles Daniel has tried to share with him.

BELIEVER: Daniel, a forty-three-year-old man. Daniel earned a business degree in college, but he was not a Christian at the time. He has been a Christian for four years, and while he has grown quickly, he is far from being an accomplished theologian. However, he has learned the value of thoughtful questions.

❖ ❖ ❖

PHIL: Hey, Daniel, did you hear about that accountant who was just arrested for embezzling funds from his clients?

DANIEL: Yes, he hurt a lot of people, didn't he?

PHIL: He sure did, including my parents. My father is hoping to retire in a couple of years, and that creep ripped him off for at least $45,000. Guys like that ought to be shot.

DANIEL: No, I give him credit for his ingenuity. It's too bad he got caught.

PHIL: What? Didn't you hear what I said? That crook stole $45,000 from my father! I can't believe you're sitting here defending him.

DANIEL: Do you think what the accountant did is wrong?

PHIL: Of course, I do. He stole from people who trusted him.

DANIEL: And that's wrong?

PHIL: I just said that.

DANIEL: But why is it wrong? You are convinced that what the man did to your father is wrong, but can you tell me why it is wrong and how you know?

PHIL: What are you talking about? Everyone knows it's wrong.

DANIEL: No, Phil, some people think they can justify stealing. If you insist it is wrong, isn't it just your opinion against theirs? And with all due respect, why should your opinion be more binding than theirs?

PHIL: It's not just my opinion, Daniel. Most people feel the same way I do, and what he did is against the law. Besides, you're the religious one. How can you disagree with me?

DANIEL: Actually, Phil, I do agree that the accountant's actions were wrong, but I reject your reasoning. You have appealed to three sources to make your case, and all three are seriously flawed. First, you based your argument on your own opinion. Second, you asserted that your view is the majority view. Third, you say that the accountant is wrong because he broke the law.

PHIL: So what's your point?

DANIEL: The point is this: Based on the criteria you are using, how would it be possible to establish wrongdoing for what the Nazis did to the Jews during the Holocaust? And if you can't make a case against the Nazis who killed millions, how can you make a case against an accountant who never killed anyone?

PHIL: Are you crazy, Daniel? First you defend the accountant, and now you say I'd be wrong for condemning those who created the Holocaust?

DANIEL: Phil, consider what you have said. If you are merely expressing your opinion, you have no leg to stand on. You are a finite creature just like the accountant. Logically, one arbitrary opinion is no different from another; therefore, it has no transcendent or binding authority. Then you appeal to majority opinion. But, Phil, do you believe the majority is always right?

PHIL: Well, not always, but in this case the majority is right.

DANIEL: Hold on, Phil. Is your last statement just an opinion? What if the accountant's opinion is that in this case the majority is wrong? You simply can't appeal to personal opinion. If you do, why can't the accountant or the Nazis do the same thing? You can't even appeal to the majority. You already admitted the majority is not always right. If we assume, for the sake of the argument, that the majority of Germans approved of the Nuremberg Laws and Hitler's treatment of the Jews, we then have all the reason we need to reject the majority. What if,

God forbid, 51 percent of Americans believed that the accountant was not wrong? What if they said that your father deserved to be robbed?

PHIL: No one steals from my father and gets away with it!

DANIEL: Fine, but you've just deprived yourself of your second argument, and rightly so.

PHIL: It doesn't matter, because the bottom line is that the accountant broke the law.

DANIEL: Phil, do you really believe that what is legal is right, or what is illegal is wrong? What do you remember about the Dred Scott decision?

PHIL: If I remember my history, it was the Supreme Court decision that ruled that a black slave had no constitutional rights because he was not a citizen.

DANIEL: Phil, do you wish to defend slavery?

PHIL: Of course not.

DANIEL: But it was legal. According to the reasoning you are using against the accountant, you would have been logically forced to defend slavery in 1857. And if you had hidden a runaway slave, you would have been helping a criminal. An appeal to human law can be dangerous, Phil.

[A period of silence ensues as Phil searches for an escape.]

PHIL: Do you mean to say the law counts for nothing?

DANIEL: No, Phil, I'm saying that human law is inadequate as an authority unless it rests upon something superior.

PHIL: What else is there? If I admit that all of my reasoning is inadequate, what am I supposed to do? Not hold the accountant responsible? You said you agreed with me that what he did was wrong.

DANIEL: That's right, Phil, but not for the same reason. Human laws are often reliable indicators of right and wrong, but only to the extent that they are consistent with a higher law, the Word of God. Phil, you may not acknowledge that higher law, but you need to see the alternative if you reject it.

[thoughtful silence]

PHIL: You know, I've never thought about it, but I'm finding it hard to counter what you're saying. Your argument seems to establish the fact that there can be no genuine standard for morals unless we root them in God. Whatever meaning or morality we claim is an arbitrary assertion, but nothing more.

DANIEL: Precisely.

PHIL: But that doesn't mean the Bible is true. Maybe there is no meaning.

DANIEL: Phil, you're halfway there. You now see where your worldview leads, a place most people would agree is unattractive. You have also acknowledged that this conclusion is inescapable, which is more than most people who hold your worldview even understand. One advantage of the Biblical worldview is that I can say that what the accountant did to your father is wrong, and I can say it without sacrificing logic or consistency. It's not my job to prove Christianity to you. You cannot please God or know Him unless it is by faith. But the faith I live by as a Christian is a reasonable faith. All people live by faith of some sort, but at some point all systems contain a logically fatal flaw, all except Christianity. I once heard a Christian teacher put it this way, "The proof of Christianity is the impossibility of the contrary. If you don't presuppose Christianity from the beginning, you cannot prove anything at all." You may not be persuaded that God is exactly Who the Bible says He is, but the real problem is with your heart and not with a lack of proof. As a matter of fact, Phil, your moral indignation over the accountant's actions shows that in your heart you have knowledge of the God Who created you. I know that someday you will stand before Him to give an account of your life. And, Phil, when you step into eternity, I hope it will be the beginning of eternity with Christ your Savior.

PHIL: Daniel, I've got some thinking to do. I don't plan on getting religious all of the sudden, but I have to admit you've made me think.

DANIEL: I'm glad to hear it, Phil. And by the way, I'll be praying for you and your father.

Summary of Phil and Daniel

The conversation between Daniel and Phil is fairly simple to follow. Phil had not been interested in what the Bible has to say. He is typical of people who want to "think for themselves" and are too busy experiencing the "real world" to take time to seriously consider the Bible. Daniel helped Phil to see that such an attitude is not as practical as it first seems. Every person has a value system with standards of right and wrong, but no person has any right to expect others to honor it unless the system is given to all of us by an authority that transcends finite man. This transcendent authority is God Himself.[1]

People may choose to reject God, but where does it leave them when they are treated unjustly by others? If right and wrong are reduced to human whims, we can ultimately expect a society to be destroyed by anarchy or oppressed by tyranny.

Daniel asked Phil two basic questions: Is it wrong? and Why? The person who has rejected God's absolutes has no way of answering these questions other than by making arbitrary assertions that can just as arbitrarily be rejected by anyone else. Ultimately only an anarchist or a tyrant can prosper under such a view. This is perhaps what Proverbs 14:12 means: "There is a way that seems right to a man, but its end is the way of death."

Remember the two basic questions: Is it wrong? and Why? In personal evangelism it is easy to create a scenario in which you can ask a person to answer these two questions. For example, you are witnessing to a woman with two young children. Try this: "Karen, if a man broke into your house, murdered your children, and robbed you, would it be wrong?" (Inevitably she will say yes.) "Why is it wrong? Isn't he free to make his own choices?"

What possible responses can Karen give? She may appeal to the law or consensus or her own opinion, but as we have seen in the encounter between Daniel and Phil, none of these appeals works. She is left with no answer, which is amazing considering the nature of the scenario. Or she has one final appeal, the Ten Commandments. If she appeals to the Bible, then you can help her see that she can't pick and choose the parts she likes (Karen can't use the law when it serves her purposes yet reject the Lawgiver and His redemptive plan.)

If Karen does not appeal to the Ten Commandments, she might appeal to the Golden Rule, "Do unto others as you would have them do unto you." But perhaps the criminal is bent on self-destruction and in his own warped way is living the Golden Rule. Besides, an appeal to the Golden Rule also places her under the authority of the Bible.

All Americans, whether Christians or not, should be terrified by the current philosophy of law that dominates most law schools, where future legislators and judges are being trained. The prevailing theory of law is legal positivism, which rejects the Christian view of law and rights upon which our nation was founded. Legal positivism teaches that law does not come from God; it comes from the state and is given its authority by the state's ability to back it up by force. As the encounter between Phil and Daniel demonstrates, legal positivism cannot withstand close scrutiny, but modern man still prefers it over God's authority.

It is important to note that when Daniel admitted he could not prove the God of the Bible, he meant that he could not change Phil's heart or disposition. Many arguments for Christian truth can be objectively true, but sinful people often remain unpersuaded because of rebellion. In that sense someone might believe that Babe Ruth was really from the planet Kryptonite. I have objectively valid arguments against this proposition, but such a person might remain unpersuaded. The fault is not with the argument but with the person who refuses to relinquish demonstrable error.

Consider the example of the Sanhedrin in Acts 4:13–17. They admitted among themselves that the apostles had really performed a miracle (a miracle by rigid Biblical standards, not the watered-down use of the term as it is often used today). Even so, they still conspired to suppress the truth rather than submit to it.

God does not ask us to change hearts—that is His job. He does ask us to speak the truth in love (Eph. 4:15) and proclaim salvation through Jesus Christ.

Thinking It Through

1. How did Daniel incorporate the truth found in Proverbs 14:12 into his questions?
2. What do Judges 17:6, 19:1, and 21:25 add to our understanding of the dangers of reducing morality to individual choices?
3. Although Phil might not be ready to accept their authority, what Scripture passages could you share with him to estab-

lish the sinfulness of the accountant's actions?

4. Daniel sought to undermine Phil's reliance upon human law unless it is founded upon God's law. What does Romans 13:1-5 teach about human law? How does this fit with Acts 5:29?

5. Phil did not immediately accept Daniel's argument even though it was valid. As has been noted, people often choose to suppress the truth rather than yield to it. (Note the example of the Sanhedrin in Acts 4:13-17.) Can you think of other Scripture passages that explain why people suppress the truth? What can we learn from Matthew 28:11-15 and Romans 1:18-21?

6. What would you say to a Christian who doubts the usefulness of evangelism and apologetics because of the hardness of the human heart? What verses would you use to correct and encourage him?

7. Think of someone you personally know who is not a Christian. Based on what you know about him, think of either a real or fictional scenario of a moral issue about which he would feel strongly.

8. On what basis do you think he would argue for his position?

9. Does he believe moral absolutes exist?
   If yes, how would he justify that belief?
   If no, how would he justify his moral outrage over the proposed scenario?

10. What questions would you ask him to help him see the weakness of his position?

11. How would you make use of this process to build a bridge to the gospel?

Notes

1. Please see appendix F (p. 253) for a summary of ethics. We are not making the claim that non-Christians have no ethics. Numerous ethical systems have been devised by non-Christians over the centuries, and all of them contain some elements of truth. The problem is that close examination exposes them as lacking any enduring foundation. Any truth these systems contain is a reflection of God's common grace in the hearts of all people, even those who deny God.

ENCOUNTER 2

THE ANIMAL RIGHTS ADVOCATE

UNBELIEVER: Linda, a thirty-six-year-old woman. Linda has embraced a radical view of animal rights, a view which, besides growing in popularity, has serious ramifications for the place of man in the world.

BELIEVER: Becky, a thirty-eight-year-old mother. Becky's children are active in their local 4-H club. The children have entered their pet rabbits at the annual county fair, where Linda and those who share her worldview have been known to confront parents and children.

❖ ❖ ❖

LINDA: I wonder how you would like to be kept in a cage all of your life. Those animals have rights, too, you know.

BECKY: They do?

LINDA: Yes, they do. And somebody has to fight to protect these animals. It is simply barbaric that they are exploited for food, fur, and entertainment.

BECKY: My children work hard every day to make sure that their animals are clean and well fed and are given proper care.

LINDA: That still doesn't make it right. All you are doing is teaching your kids how to exploit the environment.

BECKY: Actually, I'm teaching them to have dominion over the environment, which implies stewardship, not exploitation. Would you like to discuss these things?

LINDA: I certainly would! I can't believe you can stand here and use the word "dominion" when speaking of the environment and animals. It's people like you who are the worst when it comes to denying these poor animals their rights.

BECKY: Since you have brought up the issue of rights, may I ask you to explain something to me?

LINDA: Okay.

BECKY: I have four questions, but they're all related. What is a right in general? What are animals rights in particular? Where do these rights come from? And how do you know?

LINDA: [*somewhat taken aback*] You don't know what a right is? Everyone knows that.

BECKY: I want to make sure I understand your point of view. Would you be so kind as to explain it to me?

LINDA: A right is the way something deserves to be treated. Animals have a right to be free and left alone by humans. They don't deserve to be kept in cages, worn for clothes, or eaten by people.

BECKY: There is some truth in a part of your answer, and I would like to come back to it, but what about my other two questions? Where do rights come from, and how do you know?

LINDA: What do you mean, Where do they come from?

BECKY: Well, you talk about rights as though they really exist, and you claim to have the authority to tell others what these rights are, so I simply want to know where they come from and how you know what you know.

LINDA: Okay, I'll answer your question. They come from decency, compassion, common sense, and fairness. You wouldn't want to be caged, hunted, or killed for your skin. Therefore, you have no right to do such things to other animals.

BECKY: I'm an animal?

LINDA: Yes, we all are. But that's no insult. Being part of nature is a beautiful thing.

BECKY: If, for the sake of argument, I grant that I am an animal, what's wrong with eating other animals? Wolves, tigers, eagles, and thousands of other species of animals are also predators. Am I not exercising my own rights as an animal?

LINDA: Well, you eat meat as a choice. It's not a matter of survival like it is for other animals. The eating of meat by humans is the highest form of oppression.

BECKY: Why does it matter?

LINDA: If you don't need it to survive, you are not entitled to it.

BECKY: Give me your purse.

LINDA: What?

BECKY: Hand over your purse. You can survive without it. You may prefer to have it, but you're just being selfish and oppressive in your choice. The Boy Scouts have a recycling bin. Let's give them your purse and see how much of it can be recycled. After all, you told me that since eating meat isn't necessary for my survival, I was not entitled to it. You certainly won't die if I take your purse, so you are not entitled to it. Isn't that what you said?

LINDA: That's totally different.

BECKY: Why?

LINDA: Be serious. My purse isn't an animal; it doesn't have rights. It's my property.

BECKY: Purses have rights. It's cruel for you to exploit them by making them carry your belongings. How would you like it if someone forced you to carry their things? Are you an advocate of slavery?

LINDA: Listen, if you can't take this seriously, don't waste my time.

BECKY: But I am serious. I'm trying to understand your view of rights. Remember, you approached me and accused me of violating animal rights. You have told me purses don't have rights because they aren't animals, but you haven't told me how you know this. Why does one thing have a right, while another thing does not?

LINDA: There's a world of difference between a living creature like these poor rabbits and something inanimate like my purse. Everyone knows that rights only apply to living things.

BECKY: Like lice?

LINDA: Pardon me?

BECKY: Please don't be offended. I'm not being sarcastic, and I'm not making fun, but if you had lice in your hair, would you use special shampoo to kill them, or would you let them live and breed there? They are no threat to your survival, so why would you threaten theirs?

LINDA: I've never had lice.

BECKY: But what would you do if you did?

LINDA: There's a big difference between lice and rabbits or lice and mink.

BECKY: Who gets to say where to draw the line? I suspect that somewhere in the world we could find someone who would defend lice as passionately as you defend rabbits. And what if someone really believed that purses have rights and rejected your distinction between animate and inanimate objects? That might sound absurd, and you know what? It is! But that's my point. Your view of rights leads to absurdity because it is subjective. It isn't built on a reliable or objective foundation. So when someone talks about lice and purses, you might disagree, but you have no reliable ultimate authority to which you can appeal. And you know what's really scary? Your view can't justify human rights either, and where does that leave you if someone not only wants your purse but is willing to kill you in the process of taking it?

LINDA: He has no right to my purse or my life.

BECKY: I agree with you. He doesn't have that right. A few minutes ago you said a right is the way someone deserves to be treated. You have a right to life and to private property. The problem is you can't account for these rights. If you appeal to common sense or fairness, you are appealing to standards that are subjective. Other people can just as easily appeal to their own subjective standards, which might be very different from yours, whether you're talking about rabbits, purses, lice, or people!

LINDA: If you're so all-knowing, then you tell me where rights come from.

BECKY: I'd be happy to, but first let me introduce myself. My name is Becky. And you are . . .

LINDA: Linda.

BECKY: It's nice to meet you, Linda, and I want you to know that I appreciate your willingness to act upon your beliefs. I do think there is a perfect source of truth for knowing what a right is, where it comes from, and how it applies to a person's life. But, Linda, I want you to understand that even if you don't like my answer, it's the only one that doesn't end in hopeless confusion. We must either accept it or give up all hope of making sense of rights. And once we reach that point, there's nothing to stop the slaughter of entire races of people. You feel strongly about the existence of rights, and well you should. God has instilled within you a sense of rights, but you have both misconstrued how and where those rights are to be applied, and, most importantly, you have denied the God Who created all things and is the author of rights. How's that for a sweeping claim? [*Becky says this with a smile.*] Linda, would you allow me a couple of minutes to explain what I am talking about?

LINDA:　Go ahead, I'm listening.

BECKY:　The place to begin is in the beginning, and that's Genesis chapter 1 . . .

Summary of Becky and Linda

Linda is like many people in the sense that she believes in rights but can't ultimately account for them. Her standard for rights (specifically animal rights but ultimately all rights in general) is subjective. In other words, she has no fixed, universal, authoritative standard to which she can appeal. When Becky applies logic (in the spirit of Proverbs 14:12 and 26:4 and 5) to Linda's subjectivism, she is able to show that rabbits, purses, lice, and people are all in the same pool of confusion. Thus she applied Proverbs 26:5, "Answer a fool according to his folly, lest he be wise in his own eyes." If human rights are reduced to subjective standards such as social norms, intuition, human legislation, and so forth, then anything can be justified (extermination or enslavement of races, experimentation on pregnant women, drilling holes in the heads of live babies and suctioning out their brains, denying disabled people food and water, and endless other issues). Here we see the truth of Proverbs 14:12, "There is a way that seems right to a man, but its end is the way of death."[1]

Only God's Word can provide a true and absolute standard of human rights. The Bible also establishes standards for how men are to relate to the world of nature around them. Because

God created, owns, and sustains the universe, He is the author of rights, and He has revealed them by His Word. If God is not presupposed at the outset, then any talk of rights will ultimately be unintelligible.

It is important for Christians to understand the nature of human rights. The Declaration of Independence correctly rooted human rights in the creative will of God when it said, "We hold these truths to be self-evident, that all men are created equal, that they are endowed by their Creator with certain inalienable Rights." Although the Declaration is not a perfect document, it recognizes that human rights are not a gift from society or from government (in which case they could be arbitrarily revoked) but come from God. As Christians we understand that ultimately human rights come from the fact that God created mankind in His image (Gen. 1:27; 9:4–6). As Creator, God alone has the prerogative to declare what rights will be recognized. The majority of Americans are so secular in their thinking that they don't acknowledge or understand this truth, nor do they see the folly of their secularism.

In contemporary culture, discussion of rights is common. Actually, it might be better to say that the assertion of rights is common, since precious little analytical discussion seems to take place. It can be distressing to hear the claims being made under the banner of rights. Homosexuality, same-sex marriage, physician-assisted suicide, abortion on demand—these are just a few examples of how immorality is justified as a right. To make things worse, it appears that one of the few rights we don't have is to call these things sin. The present state of affairs can be a blessing, however, in the same sense in which we said immorality can be a blessing (see chapter 4).

Since rights are so important to people, we should actively look for opportunities to engage unbelievers in the type of conversation Becky used. Becky's use of questions was consistent with ATW. Non-Christian worldviews cannot truly account for human rights (and the proper place of animals), ethics, science, and reason itself. Becky brought Linda to the place where Linda was willing to have the Biblical worldview explained to her. Whether or not Linda yields to it is between her and God. Of course, our greatest desire is for the unbeliever to yield to the gospel message and be saved. However, we must always remember that the gospel message is included within the larger body of truth, which is the Christian worldview contained within the Scriptures.

Do you see how Becky's building a bridge to Linda could lead to the gospel? One way would be to assure Linda that as the creator, God is interested in how people treat animals. Better news still: God cares about people. Linda can be in right relationship with nature, but she first has to enter into a right relationship with the God Who is over all nature. Becky can also show Linda Romans 8:19–23. Now that's grounds for an exciting presentation of the gospel!

Thinking It Through

Americans believe in all sorts of rights. The exercise of rights is a daily part of political, social, and moral dialogue in our culture. Christians need to understand the source and the foundation upon which genuine rights stand. Only then can we engage unbelievers by using ATW. How would you answer these questions?

1. Do humans have rights? If so, from where do they come, and how do you know?
2. What do Genesis 1:27 and 9:4–6 say about mankind?
3. I believe that mankind's rights derive from bearing the image of God, and from man's unique status in the created world. As Creator, God alone has the authority to declare what rights will be recognized. Why is murder a violation of the

victims rights? Because every human bears the image of God, and the murder would be sin against God. A person's rights are rooted in God's creative purposes. Do you agree or disagree with this assessment? Why?

4. Is there a connection between the Ten Commandments (Exodus 20:1–17) and human rights? If so, what is it?

5. Do animals have rights? Why or why not? How would you answer this question Biblically?

6. I believe that animals do not have rights because they lack the necessary prerequisite of bearing the image of God. Genesis 9:2–6 draws a clear distinction between mankind and animals. Although humans may have God-given responsibilities toward animals (Prov. 12:10), animals themselves have no inherent rights (at least not in the same sense as human rights). Do you agree or disagree with this assessment? Why?

7. What does Genesis 1:28 teach about mankind's responsibilities toward animals and the environment? If Genesis implies that man, as the image-bearer of God, rules as God's representative, what are our duties as stewards?

8. What does Romans 8:19–22 teach about God's redemptive plans for the created world? How could you use this passage with Linda to build a bridge to the gospel? Hint: God's redemptive plan includes the environment that Linda so dearly loves. God saves the sweetest aspect of redemption for sinners, of whom Linda is one.

Notes

1. Have you ever wondered why it is that some people take animal rights to an extreme? I am not referring to people who love their pets, or the common decency of not wanting to see an animal suffer needlessly. The discussion of animal rights takes us, once again, to the shores of postmodernism. The historic Christian worldview that at one

time dominated the West recognized that God is the center of the universe. The Enlightenment, which gave birth to the modern era, took God off the throne and replaced Him with man. Now that modernism is being eclipsed by postmodernism, there must be a corresponding transition on the throne. God has already been dethroned, now man is being dethroned. What else remains? Many animal rights activists are simply one manifestation of the postmodern era. And since animals lack any oppressive agendas of their own, they become candidates for the empty throne.

ENCOUNTER 3

THE EVOLUTIONIST

UNBELIEVER: Dr. Madelyn Skinner, a college science professor. Dr. Skinner is committed to a materialistic view of nature. In other words, she believes that only the material, natural universe exists and that there is no evidence to support belief in a supernatural God or that the immaterial human soul can exist apart from the natural body.

BELIEVER: Jonathan, a Christian student. He is not a science major, but he understands that there is as much philosophy in science class as there is science. Jonathan is going to ask Dr. Skinner to justify her use of reason. In other words, is it reasonable for her to use reason? If her concept of the universe is correct, she might have trouble justifying herself. Observe closely as Jonathan asks Professor Skinner some questions that might be new to her.

JONATHAN: Dr. Skinner, you have been adamant in this class that you reject the teachings of those who believe in a special creative act by God. Why do you feel so strongly about this?

SKINNER: Because I am a scientist, and there is no room in science for fairy tales. The discoveries we have made have eliminated the need for religious crutches. Science has brought us out of the Dark Ages. We can now explain life by the totally natural process of evolution.

JONATHAN: But how does providing an explanation automatically make that explanation true?

SKINNER: All of the evidence demonstrates that evolution is true.

JONATHAN: So you accept naturalistic evolution because it is reasonable?

SKINNER: Not only is it reasonable, but the alternative—Adam and Eve and the apple tree—is ludicrous. I do not mean to offend, but those things simply don't belong in a science class.

JONATHAN: Why does reason matter? Why do we need to use reason?

SKINNER: Jonathan, that question seems out of character for you. Are you being sarcastic? Because if so, it is not appreciated.

JONATHAN: No, Dr. Skinner, I'm not being sarcastic at all. You have stated that reason is central to science. I want to know why it is so important.

SKINNER: Now Jonathan, certainly you can see that if we did not use reason, we would have no way of conducting experiments, investigating evidence, and understanding how nature operates.

JONATHAN: Dr. Skinner, I think this next question is the most serious question I can ask. Where does reason come from?

CLASSMATE: Hey, Jonathan, philosophy class is down the hall.

JONATHAN: Yes, but this question is directly related to science.

SKINNER: Well, Jonathan, to answer your question I would simply say that reason is a function of the brain, and it is a useful survival mechanism. Through the eons of evolutionary time the human ability to reason has served us well.

JONATHAN: Doesn't that view imply that reason does nothing to discover truth? If so, can evolution ever be shown to be true? It seems that using reason should lead us to conclude that nothing in science is true.

SKINNER: Okay, class, I won't give you the quiz today, so you can relax and quit stalling for time [*cheers abound*]. Jonathan, what exactly is your point?

JONATHAN: I'm carrying your assertions to their logical conclusion. Haven't you said that all of life is the result of time and chance acting on matter?

SKINNER: Yes, I have, along with about a million other legitimate scientists.

JONATHAN: If you're right, then in this totally material, non-supernatural world that is the result of time, chance, and matter, reason is nothing more than an electrochemical reaction that occurs in the brain. When a scientist observes a chemical reaction in a test tube, he doesn't say that the chemical reaction is true or false; it just is. If I assert that evolution is true, am I not simply acting on a chemical reaction in my brain, which is itself the result of a random combination of time, chance, and matter?

SKINNER: You make reason sound unimportant.

JONATHAN: I'm not denigrating reason. I'm relying on it. What I'm saying is my use of reason is valid if and only if I reject your naturalistic evolution. Your use of reason is valid only if you first assume a creationist foundation.

SKINNER: How can you possibly accuse science of being contrary to reason? If it were not for our use of reason, we never could have made so many advances and discoveries. And having said that, let me make myself clear: I am not a creationist.

JONATHAN: I don't deny science has used reason. That would be denying the obvious. What I am trying to determine is how scientists with your view of mankind and the brain can avoid serious inconsistency in using reason, especially when you make statements such as "this is true" or "that is false." For example, when you say, "Naturalistic evolution is a fact established by science," aren't you, according to your beliefs, simply experiencing an electrochemical reaction of some kind in your brain?

SKINNER: An electrochemical process, yes. Simple? No. It is the very complexity of the thought process that enables us to discover truth.

JONATHAN: Whether we call it simple or complex, a chemical reaction is still neither true nor false; it just is. Suppose that at the same time you are having a chemical reaction I am also having one, and mine prompts me to say, "Naturalistic evolution is patently false. All of life is to be attributed to a Creator-God." If all the activities of thought are solely chemical activities of the brain, an organ that is nothing more than the result of time and chance acting on matter over eons of time, then how can one chemical reaction be truer than any other? They are not true or false; they just are. When an intelligent scientist such as you uses reason and expects others to subscribe to that reason, you are engaging in an activity that your own view of mankind renders illegitimate. For you to use reason, you must set aside your naturalistic science and rely upon God.

SKINNER: Your opinion in the area shows naiveté, Jonathan, although I am glad my students are trying to be thoughtful. Before I show you why you are wrong, though, I am curious as to what you meant when you say I must rely on God to use reason. What do you mean by that?

JONATHAN: The Bible teaches that the human mind's ability to reason has been given to us by God. Being created in the image of God is the thing that allows meaningful communication, comprehension, and reasoning to take place. Dr. Skinner, when you use reason you are exercising a God-given ability even though you deny its origin. If we reject this premise, we are left with a human brain that is nothing more than a collection of molecules that have chemical reactions, none superior or inferior to another, none more true or less true than another. How can we logically even classify chemical reactions into those categories? When we do attempt to classify chemical reactions into categories such as true/false, right/wrong, and so on, we are simply experiencing yet another chemical reaction that defies categorization. When you deny my line of reasoning, you are experiencing a chemical reaction that is different from mine, but why should the particular arrangement and operation of molecules in your brain be seen as true and the arrangement and operations of molecules in my brain be seen as false? It defies logic to even suggest that your molecules and chemical reactions are "truer" than mine, or that mine are "truer" than yours. No, Dr. Skinner, when you use reason it's because of how God has made you, not how blind chance, time, and matter have made you.

SKINNER: That is a most interesting argument. I'll give you credit for that. But you have made one serious error. You underestimate the power and rich complexity of evolution. To borrow a phrase, it is almost miraculous! The brain's ability to reason does not need a supernatural origin to make sense. It is really nothing more than a helpful survival mechanism. That's what evolution does. It elevates the survival mechanisms that are most advantageous and eliminates those that are not. For example, a cheetah is not as smart as a human, but it survives because it can run seventy miles per hour. A fish can't reason like us, but when it reproduces, it might produce hundreds or thousands of offspring so the species survives because of sheer numbers. One need not look any further than this

JONATHAN: to explain our ability to reason; it is a simple matter of evolution. It is nonscientific to appeal to God or a mind or soul that can exist apart from the body.

JONATHAN: Did you notice the sunset yesterday?

SKINNER: Yes, I couldn't help but notice it.

JONATHAN: What did you think about it?

SKINNER: It was beautiful.

JONATHAN: Have you seen sunsets that were less impressive than yesterday's?

SKINNER: I suppose I have. What of it?

JONATHAN: Your impression that yesterday's sunset was beautiful in comparison to other sunsets is totally meaningless. I found it to be beautiful, and I know that my statement is meaningful because God has given us the ability to make aesthetic judgments so that we can appreciate His creation. Yet such observations are totally superfluous to survival needs and therefore are meaningless, if indeed the mind is what you say it is. How about things such as love, mercy, joy, and humor? They make life pleasant, but if they are nothing more than intricate chemical reactions, they ultimately lack any true meaning or purpose. Is your love for your husband just a chemical reaction to a need to continue the species? And if it is, how did blind chance and time acting on matter produce this survival mechanism?[1] Your view of the brain is logically self-defeating. The more you try to rationalize your position, the more you demonstrate that reason is something much more than a chemical reaction in a totally naturalistic universe. Although you won't admit it, you are depending on the fact that the human mind, though related to the brain, also transcends the brain. Human beings are more than just a material entity.

SKINNER: What you are advocating is simply not to be believed, Jonathan. Your description of humans indicates a belief in some invisible soul or mind that is somehow greater than the material that comprises your body. There is not one shred of scientific evidence that such a thing exists.

JONATHAN: I think your use of the word "evidence" is unfair, but I don't want to get sidetracked right now, so I'll just ask one more question. According to the statement you just made, you reject belief in the human soul, which exists in addition to our physical bodies because it can't be proved scientifically. Is that correct?

SKINNER: Yes. I am a scientist, after all.

JONATHAN: So you accept only that which you can prove scientifically?

SKINNER: In a manner of speaking, yes.

JONATHAN: Then can you prove your statement is true scientifically?

SKINNER: What do you mean?

JONATHAN: You reject my belief in the human soul, which I believe continues to exist after the death of the body. You say that since I cannot prove my belief scientifically, you are prevented from believing it. This is because you hold as doubtful that which cannot be proved scientifically. I want to know what scientific evidence or experiment you can provide that proves the statement, "Only that which can be proved scientifically is true." Your foundation reflects your philosophy. It is not in and of itself a scientific statement. Isn't your starting point both a step of faith and a contradiction?

ANOTHER
CLASSMATE: I get it. It's like saying there are no absolutes. If there are no absolutes then that itself is an absolute, and so you are contradicting yourself. If you believe only that which can be proved scientifically, you have no way of proving your premise scientifically; therefore, you can't believe your own premise.

JONATHAN: That's close enough to what I'm saying. The premise or presupposition that says we will accept only as true that which can be established scientifically becomes incoherent when it is applied against itself. There is nothing wrong with presuppositions; we all have them. But when they lead to self-contradictions, should we continue to use them?

ANOTHER
CLASSMATE: But ultimately you are being antiscientific. Without science we'd still be in the Dark Ages.

JONATHAN: Science did not deliver us from the so-called Dark Ages. Science is a tool that, when properly used, can be beneficial. But it is a mistake to think of science as the most basic discipline. The word "beneficial" is beyond the realm of science—it requires a judgment more basic than science. Science is built upon philosophy. All scientists bring a philosophy into their work, whether they are aware of it or not. Some of you are majoring in science because you believe science is good. But to discuss the concept of good is doing philosophy or theology, not science. Philosophy can exist without modern science, but science cannot exist without philosophy or theology. Much of what we are taught is strongly influenced by the teacher's philosophy. There's nothing wrong with that, but the philosophy ought to be out in the open and subject to investigation. I appreciate Dr. Skinner for allowing this discussion to take place.

SKINNER: Let's remember this is a biology course. Perhaps we'll talk about these things again before the semester is over, but tomorrow you will definitely be having a quiz!

Summary of Jonathan and Dr. Skinner

Although this was a fairly involved encounter, Jonathan limited his questions to two basic areas. His questions were designed to help his classmates and Dr. Skinner see the problems that arise when people appeal to scientific knowledge without first acknowledging a dependence upon God as creator. He argued as follows:

1. Human reason is a purely material process involving electrochemical processes within the brain.
2. Naturally occurring chemical reactions cannot be categorized as true or false; they simply are.

Therefore: There is no valid reason for thinking that human reasoning is true.

By framing the argument in this manner, Jonathan has attempted to demonstrate that when carried over into science, human intellectual autonomy creates questions with which science cannot cope. Dr. Skinner was quick to point out that reasoning is a survival mechanism and is typical of how evolution works. However, Jonathan did not argue that reason is useless; he instead demonstrated that human reason cannot discover truth (or even talk about truth) if it is jettisoned from submission to God. It also means that concepts such as right, wrong, justice, beauty, love, mercy, and so forth have no ultimate meaning. Obviously Jonathan does believe that proper reasoning can lead to truth, but he has pointed out that only someone with a Biblical worldview can logically view reason in this manner. Since the atheist (materialist) must borrow from theism to correctly use reason, it means that his rejection of God is without reason! The Christian claim is not that non-Christians can't use concepts such as truth, beauty, love, justice, and so forth. Our claim is that they can't truly account for their use of these things. Their own worldview cannot provide the necessary preconditions for these concepts to be intelligible. Unbelievers cannot escape God, and they show their reliance upon God every time they use the God-given abilities they have.

This encounter touches on what has been called the "mind-body problem." How do humans think, and what is the relationship between their thoughts and their physical bodies? Are they identical? (Are thoughts purely a physical process that occurs in the brain?) Or is there a distinction between the human brain and the human mind? Obviously the Christian answer is yes, there is a distinction. We know that human consciousness continues after the death of the body (2 Cor. 5:6–8). A helpful discussion of these issues can be found in J. P. Moreland's *Scaling the Secular City: A Defense of Christianity* (Grand Rapids: Baker Book House, Grand Rapids, 1987). This is an issue worth studying. Some Christian apologists would claim that questions about the human mind and the inadequacy of purely materialistic explanations supply one of the strongest arguments for the existence of God.[2]

The second trap some people have fallen into is placing too

much confidence in scientific proof. Jonathan pointed out that there is a contradiction in asserting that only things proven scientifically should be accepted as true. After all, what scientific proof can establish this basic premise? Obviously there are areas of knowledge that lie beyond the scope of science (life after death, an immaterial God, and so on). Those who dismiss God on scientific grounds are giving science more authority than it can possibly merit, and they must also deny many other nonscientific truths, such as the existence of beauty, justice, and value.

Jonathan knew these things when he began the conversation, but by asking questions he was able to prompt his classmates and teacher to think with a perspective previously overlooked or ignored. Do not underestimate the prevalence and the blind dogmatism of people who worship at the altar of modern scientific knowledge. It is a mind-set that is a serious barrier when presenting truth about spiritual matters. Remember, all knowledge that stands in opposition to God is flawed. The Christian should point out the flaw so that the unbeliever is confronted with the error of human autonomy.

Thinking It Through

1. Can you think of a way to tie Psalm 19:1-4 in with this encounter?
2. If Romans 1:18-20 is true, why are there people who believe like Dr. Skinner?
3. Some Christians have tried to reconcile the creation account of Genesis with the modern theory of evolution. By combining the two, they have come up with what is called theistic evolution. Do you believe that the Bible allows for such a synthesis? Why or why not?
4. I believe that arguing with an evolutionist solely on evidential grounds ignores the fact that both sides are wearing worldview sunglasses that control their interpretation of scientific

data. (See appendixes A and B, pages 209 and 217.) Certainly there is a place for debating the data, but how did Jonathan manage to direct the conversation in a way that other non-scientists can imitate?

5. Many committed evolutionists believe that the gospel is irrelevant and meaningless in our scientifically advanced era. How could Jonathan use ATW with Dr. Skinner to build a bridge to the gospel?

6. What do Romans 1:16 and Hebrews 4:12 teach about the possibility of having an effective witness to an evolutionist, even if you are not trained in science?

Notes

1. Because this encounter is taking place in a science classroom, the conversation has included comments on the role of chance in creating certain outcomes. The truth of the matter is that chance does not exist; therefore, it has no causal power. What does this mean? One of the best books available on this topic is R. C. Sproul's *Not A Chance: The Myth of Chance in Modern Science and Cosmology* (Grand Rapids: Baker Book House, 1994). Naturalistic science must not be given a pass on its misleading and unwarranted appeals to chance as a causal explanation.

2. In recent years some members of the scientific community have stepped up the intensity of their attacks on Christian theism. They base their attacks on what they claim are advances in our knowledge of the brain's operation, evolution, and genetics. If you are unfamiliar with the latest literature, you would be shocked at the "evangelistic" fervor of these critics. I suspect that part of this fervor is a desperate attempt to undermine the Christian claim that scientific naturalism completely fails when called upon to give an account of morality and ethics. These scientists do not speak for the entire scientific community, but their influence and their dedication must be taken seriously. It is this same community of atheistic scientists who fights so militantly against any mention of Intelligent Design in public schools.

ENCOUNTER 4

THE POSTMODERNIST

UNBELIEVER: Tina, a university student who has a postmodernist view of history and the world. As longs as she holds onto her worldview, she will not only reject the gospel, she will be offended by its exclusive truth claims.

BELIEVER: Dr. Carter, a history professor at Tina's university. He is aware of her beliefs and understands that there is a great gulf between Tina and him. In Christian compassion he is going to try to reach her in an unusual way. Dr. Carter wants to help Tina look beyond her own worldview and consider the gospel of Jesus Christ. He has recently returned a research paper Tina submitted and has given her an F. Let's see what happens next.

TINA: Dr. Carter, you have no right to give me an F on my research paper. I showed this paper to my academic advisor, and she agrees with me. I have a meeting with the departmental chairperson this afternoon, and I am going to lodge an official complaint.

DR. CARTER: Tina, why do you think I gave you an F?

TINA: Because you're intolerant, Dr. Carter. It's obvious in the way you teach history. Your views are Eurocentric and racist. Your lectures are filled with the teachings of fascist men who oppressed everyone who refused to think like them, including women, the working class, and minorities. They oppressed anyone they viewed as radical or a threat to the status quo.

DR. CARTER: Well, Tina, I do have a philosophy of life that guides how I teach history. Do you think this standard is wrong?

TINA: The problem with you, Dr. Carter, is that you're the product of rationalism, a rationalism defined by those in power. I suspected as much when I heard you were invited to speak at a Christian meeting on campus. You are holding onto a dead orthodoxy. The arrogance of Christianity's message is offensive to me. You have no right to judge people who don't agree with you, whether they be feminists, gays, vegans, or neo-pagans. We are a threat to you, and you know we're winning. So you resort to giving me an F, even though I deserve an A.

DR. CARTER: Yes, I did write F on your paper, Tina, but before we talk any further, there's something I want to show you. If you will look here on my screen, I want to show you your grade for this paper and for the course.

[Tina sees her grade.]

TINA: An *A*? I don't get it. When you gave my paper back, it had an F on it.

DR. CARTER: Tina, let's just say I was using an unorthodox teaching method when I wrote F on your paper. Your paper was excellent. I knew it would be even before I read it because you're one of my best students. I admire you for many reasons. I know this course has been difficult for you because your view of history differs from mine. You've not been afraid to speak your mind, and I wouldn't want you to be any other way. You've worked hard to master the course material, even though you have disagreed with my views. I have given you an A because you deserve it, but I wrote F on your paper because I wanted to make you think. Now, Tina, if I had truly given you an F, why would that have been wrong?

[Dr. Carter asks this question with a smile, which Tina returns. Her hard edge is gone, and now her curiosity takes over.] yeah right

TINA: Okay, I know this is one of your trick questions, so I am going to be real careful. My basic answer would be that the course syllabus has a set of requirements, and that I have met and surpassed each one. According to the syllabus I have earned an A. On top of that, it's your syllabus, so you should be willing to abide by it—am I close?

DR. CARTER: You sound unsure.

TINA: If I sound unsure, it's because you've freaked me out!

[They both laugh.]

DR. CARTER: What if I said that there really is no difference between an A and an F? They both mean the same thing.

TINA: But they aren't the same.

DR. CARTER: Okay, try this one on for size. I gave you an F because it's what I really wanted to do. I know what the syllabus says, but you have to understand that the university forces me to provide a syllabus. If I had my way, I would do away with the syllabus altogether. Why should I have to accept their restrictions? Why can't I be free to run this course by standards that I can change on a whim?

TINA: Because you knew the requirements when you came here. No one made you come to this school. You chose to be here.

DR. CARTER: That's not true. I have a family to feed, and my training is as a historian. The university knows I need a job, so it has the true power in our relationship. I could leave, but where would I go? Good teaching jobs are hard to come by. I am a victim in all of this. Being forced to use a syllabus and being forced to use the university's grading scale is testimony to the fact that I am being oppressed. So if I muster up the courage to resist my oppressors, disregard the syllabus, and do what I truly want to do in my heart, why should you have a problem with that?

TINA: But the university's requirements for you are not oppressive. You have academic freedom. The standards that exist are just commonsense procedures for providing some semblance of order so that the school can function. Your attitude would lead to anarchy, not justice.

DR. CARTER: Anarchy? Tina, you sound like the oppressors. Isn't one person's anarchy another person's freedom?

TINA: But there's nothing unreasonable about the university's standards.

DR. CARTER: That's what you say. The problem with you, Tina, is that you're intolerant. You have a vested interest in preserving the status quo. Aren't you defending the university because you want to force me to give you an A regardless of how it makes me feel or what I believe?

TINA: I'm just asking you to be fair, Dr. Carter.

DR. CARTER: Fair by whose definition? Do you really think my giving you an F is unfair?

TINA: Yes. All you have to do is live by the standards you agreed to at the beginning of the semester.

DR. CARTER: But that's oppression.

[Tina is silent for several moments.]

TINA: Okay, Dr. Carter, what's your point?

DR. CARTER: Tina, I wanted to see what you really believe. I've seen it, I am impressed by it, and I agree with it.

TINA: What in the world are you talking about?

DR. CARTER: Am I being a pain in the neck?

TINA: Sort of.

DR. CARTER: To be honest with you, I was trying on your world-view. And in a sneaky way I was trying to get you to try mine on. Can I point some things out to you?

TINA: I guess so.

DR. CARTER: Tina, when you thought I had given you an F, something inside you told you that it was unjust. You appealed to the syllabus with the expectation that, as different as you and I are as individuals, we could both interpret its meaning the same way. You then differentiated between an A and an F. You are not willing to blur their distinctive identity. Letter grades have fixed meanings that set them apart from each other. Furthermore, you are certain that I am also capable of drawing the same logical conclusion you have drawn. You defended the university's standards as being fair and reasonable. There are two possible ways to look at this. Your defense may be nothing more than seeking an A for the course, in which case I was right for accusing you of being willing to play the role of the oppressor. On the other hand, you might really believe that there is a standard for fairness and reasonableness that transcends each particular individual. You therefore have legitimate grounds for rejecting my belief that I should create my own morality when it comes to grading papers. One thing I know about you, Tina, is that you sincerely hate oppression. That's how I know you would not fight for an A in this class unless you truly believed it was the right thing to do. You remind me of someone I deeply respect and admire. Can I tell you Who it is you remind me of?

TINA: Yes. [*Tina is now listening intently.*]

DR. CARTER: Would it shock you to hear that you remind me of Jesus Christ?

TINA: Are you serious?

DR. CARTER: I wouldn't say it if I didn't believe it. Jesus Christ taught many of the things you just appealed to in our conversation. He believed language can convey truth and that there is a standard of justice and fairness that we should all honor. Jesus believed that when a person gives their word like I did when I handed out the syllabus, they are obligated to keep it. Truth can be known, and it really matters.

TINA: But I don't have to be a Christian to believe the things I said. Many other religions would say the same thing, and so would a lot of agnostics.

DR. CARTER: I agree with you, Tina, but I would add an important qualifier. Although non-Christians use some of these values and perspectives, we can make sense of them only if Christianity is uniquely true.

TINA: What do you mean?

DR. CARTER: [*looking at his watch*] I'll tell you what, Tina. I'm meeting my wife for lunch over at the coffee shop. I think you would like her. I would be honored if you would come to lunch with us as my guest. We can talk about some of the questions I've raised, and I'll do my best to answer any questions you might have. Can you spare an hour?

TINA: I'd like to, but I was supposed to meet my roommate for lunch.

DR. CARTER: Bring her along.

TINA: Are you sure?

DR. CARTER: Absolutely. We'll see you in about twenty minutes. But for now, give me back your paper for a second.

[Tina hands her research paper to Dr. Carter.]

Dr. Carter: This was one of the best papers I received, Tina. *[He crosses out the F and writes A with a large red marker.]* Fair enough?

TINA: Fair enough!

Summary of Dr. Carter and Tina

Dr. Carter was aware of Tina's postmodern mind-set. Her complaints about his approach to history are common ones in contemporary academia. Dr. Carter had three goals in his encounter with Tina. First, he wanted to interact with her innate sense of justice. Tina cannot escape the way God has made her. Second, Dr. Carter wanted to make use of the way God has made the world in which both Dr. Carter and Tina live. His use of language (the meaning of the letters A and F) reflects the existence of fixed universal meanings. Third, Dr. Carter wanted to build a personal bridge to Tina where a relationship could take hold. The invitation to lunch accomplished this goal.

I believe the Christian worldview can interact rationally and logically with postmodernism. Is this because postmodernism accepts Christian categories of thought? No. But since we believe Christianity is true, we accept what it says about human nature. Tina is created in the image of God. Her fallen sin nature makes her a rebel in God's universe and leaves her spiritually dead (Eph. 2:1-3), but the image of God within her has not been destroyed. This is why she can exhibit an awareness of justice and injustice.

God has also created language. Language accomplishes what

God intended for it despite fallen humanity's best efforts to distort and confuse it. Tina was not about to abandon the law of identity (a function of logic). She knew that receiving an F was fundamentally not the same as receiving an A. She was ready to impose this conviction upon Dr. Carter as though his individual perspective was also bound to the same meaning of A and F that she has. Was she acting as a tyrant? No. She was simply functioning in the world God has created. Without realizing it she was acting like a person created in the image of God.

Notice how Dr. Carter did not react in anger when Tina attacked his view of history. Christians have always had a God-given obligation to be loving and compassionate toward those who hate us. But in today's world this is even more important than ever before. Perhaps the best apologetic of all is when Christians manifest the love of God toward others (2 Cor. 5:14–20).

Many Christian scholars today are proposing a whole new model for apologetics in a postmodern world. They emphasize personal relationships as being able to accomplish what logical argumentation cannot do. Consider Peter's command in 1 Peter 3:15 to be ready always to give a reason for the hope that is within us. When was the last time a non-Christian asked you about the hope you have within you? In other words, Christians should be so filled with God's love and the supernatural joy, peace, and contentment He gives that non-Christians will be amazed and puzzled by what they see in us. Peter assumed that Christians, though being aliens and strangers in this world (1 Pet. 2:11), will nevertheless be in relationships with non-Christians so they can see the difference in us.

The heightened emphasis on relational apologetics or lifestyle evangelism is essential, but I do not believe it should replace rational apologetics, however. Rather than seeing it is as an either/or choice, we should see it as both/and. Only this approach takes into account the Biblical call to interact with people on a rational basis (Acts 17:16, 17) and on a relational level (Matt. 9:10–13).

Dr. Carter and his wife are going to share their faith in Christ with Tina and her roommate over lunch. Will Tina receive the truth? Only God knows. But Dr. Carter has built both an intellectual and a relational bridge to Tina. He has engaged postmodernism without surrendering Christian distinctives. We can do the same.

Thinking It Through

1. Tina criticized Dr. Carter's commitment to rationalism. Unfortunately, many Christian are moving in Tina's direction. We see this trend in the relegating of theology to a place of unimportance. What is the proper role of reason and logic in the Christian worldview? What Scripture passages help answer this question?

2. Dr. Carter pointed out that both he and Tina understand the difference between an A and an F. How does this understanding reflect that they are both created in God's image?

3. How did Dr. Carter bring the conversation around to Jesus Christ? How could he take the conversation to the next step of sharing the gospel? What passages should be especially useful in this context?

4. How did Dr. Carter's encounter with Tina reflect 1 Peter 3:15?

5. Dr. Carter displayed a tender, humble spirit toward Tina. Do you believe his mannerisms are widespread among the Christians you know? What are some Scripture verses that instruct us on Christlikeness?

ENCOUNTER 5

THE LIBERAL "CHRISTIAN"

UNBELIEVER: Glenn, a man in his early fifties. Glenn attends a theologically liberal church that denies several historic Christian doctrines because they are viewed as outdated, prescientific, and fundamentalist. Glenn joins his church in denying these doctrines that are essential to Biblical faith.

BELIEVER: Sean, also in his early fifties and Glenn's cousin. Sean is a born-again Christian who understands that his cousin Glenn is still lost in his sin and needs to be saved and needs to embrace the true historic gospel message of the Bible. The subject of church initiates this encounter.

❖ ❖ ❖

GLENN: We really enjoy our church, and our pastor is wonderful. She's in tune with the modern world.

121

SEAN: That's fine, but what if the world is out of tune?

GLENN: What do you mean by that?

SEAN: Consider this, Glenn. If I wanted to learn how to sing, I would go to a music teacher. Now this teacher has a piano that he uses to teach me the musical notes. I learn to match the notes coming from the piano, and after a while I can sing in perfect harmony with the piano. But what if the piano is badly out of tune?

GLENN: You would be in agreement with the piano, but your singing would actually be out of tune.

SEAN: That's right. The problem is that I would not know that I was out of tune. I'd be using the wrong standard by which to judge my singing, and the whole time I would be assuming my singing was correct.

GLENN: So what are you trying to imply?

SEAN: You admire your pastor's ministry, and I am willing to assume that she is trying hard to make her community a better place.

GLENN: She certainly is!

SEAN: But what if she's attempting to match an out-of-tune piano?

GLENN: What?

SEAN: You said she's in tune with the modern world. But are you sure the modern world is in tune? Because if it isn't, then doesn't that mean your pastor will be just as out of tune as the world is?

GLENN: Sean, you don't even know my pastor. Who are you to criticize her?

SEAN: It's not your pastor I'm challenging. It is the standards of this world that I find wanting. They should not be imitated; they should be rejected.

GLENN: I've got to tell you, Sean, that you and I definitely part company when it comes to this whole area. Your thinking is too rigid. I know your church is one of those fundamentalist churches, but you shouldn't take every verse in the Bible so literally.

SEAN: In Colossians 2:8 the apostle Paul was clearly speaking literally when he condemned thinking that is contrary to God's truth.

GLENN: Listen, the Bible is an inspiring piece of literature. Once you peel away the myths and errors, you can find some real gems. That's what I so enjoy about my pastor. She doesn't get sidetracked with all the fundamentalist negatives.

SEAN: And negatives are bad?

GLENN: Yes.

SEAN: Some of the Ten Commandments are framed in negative terms. Do you think the Bible should be rejected when the Ten Commandments condemn murder, theft, lying, and cursing?

GLENN: Perhaps some of those things are unavoidable, but we shouldn't harp on them. My real problem, however, is with the two worst negatives imaginable.

SEAN: And what are they?

GLENN: Well, I think it is arrogant to claim that only Christians get to Heaven. Also, nothing is more detestable than the doctrine of Hell. My God would never send anyone to Hell!

SEAN: So you think it is unreasonable for Christians to believe that someone must be a Christian to see Heaven, and it is unreasonable to believe in a place called Hell.

GLENN: First of all, most of the Christians I know don't believe those things. I'm a Christian, and I don't believe them. Second, it is unreasonable to believe those things. Only extremists still hold to those doctrines. I'm not attacking you personally, Sean, but there is no way I can accept your antiquated brand of Christianity.

SEAN: What is a Christian? What does the word itself mean?

GLENN: A Christian is someone who follows the teachings of Jesus Christ.

SEAN: Did Jesus Christ teach that there are many ways to Heaven? Consider John 14:6, "Jesus said to him, 'I am the way, the truth, and the life. No one comes to the Father except through Me.'" Jesus also spent more time warning people of Hell than He did promising Heaven. According to your own definition, a person who claims to be a Christian must believe the things Jesus taught. As far as dismissing these doctrines as being antiquated, are we to assume that they are true only for a time, but over the passing of years they cease to be true?

GLENN: Whoa! Slow down, cousin. Your questions imply that it is not valid for me to call myself a Christian just because I reject some outdated doctrines and refuse to get hung up on legal metaphors.

SEAN: Did you mean something different when you said a

Christian is someone who follows the teachings of
Christ?

GLENN: I do follow the teachings of Christ. He was the
perfect example of love and tolerance, and that is
what I follow. Jesus was too loving to have ever
taught the doctrine of Hell and to have said what is
written in John 14:6. Those were the opinions and
beliefs of the people who wrote the Bible. We must
weed those things out and focus on the real Jesus.

SEAN: Glenn, couldn't you be accused of holding a thoroughly unreasonable position? You say you are a
Christian, yet you reject certain Biblical doctrines
because you and others think they are unreasonable in today's world. But don't you abandon reason
to do this?

GLENN: How so?

SEAN: You reject certain doctrines as being the product of
antiquated times, no longer to be taken seriously by
reasonable modern minds.

GLENN: Yes, just like I reject the antiquated idea of a flat
earth.

SEAN: No Glenn, not "just like," for we are not talking
about a physical thing such as a planet. We are talking about something recorded in a document that
claims to be a true record of history. I can't prove
to you Hell exists, and I'm not interested in trying.
God's Word simply declares it to be, whether you
like it or not. The fact that the modern mind is re-
pelled by the doctrine of Hell does not therefore
render it untrue. When Isaac Newton provided his
explanations of the laws of planetary motion,

gravity, inertia, and so on, the scientific revolution was born, and prior ideas were rejected as outdated. The problem is that two centuries later a man by the name of Einstein came along and made Newton obsolete, at least in part, and Einstein himself predicted that someday his theories would also be overturned. Seeing how frequently one generation's modern ideas are rejected for being outdated by a later generation ought to teach us that it is unwise to appeal to current trends for our authority. Listen Glenn, I admit my analogy of Newton and Einstein is less than perfect, but it does remind me of Isaiah 40:6–8, which says "All flesh is grass, and all its loveliness is like the flower of the field. The grass withers, the flower fades, because the breath of the LORD blows upon it; surely the people are grass. The grass withers, the flower fades, but the word of our God stands forever."

GLENN: So what's your point?

SEAN: Glenn, you believe your ideas are true because they are consistent with what a modern-day enlightened person would believe. Let's say that two hundred years from now a person were to look back to our era, would it be right for them to reject your ideas just because two centuries had passed?

GLENN: No, I guess not. If what I'm saying is true, the mere passing of time will not make it false.

SEAN: In the same way, the extreme age of the Bible does not mean it is untrue. It is fallacious to appeal to the passing of time as an authoritative reason to reject certain doctrines.

GLENN: Okay, I didn't choose my words carefully enough. Let me rephrase it. The doctrines under consideration did not cease to be true because of the passing of time. They were never true to begin with; and, even more importantly, Jesus never taught them.

SEAN: How do you know Jesus didn't teach them?

GLENN: Because the real Jesus was loving and tolerant. He would not have promoted such horrible ideas. We must peel away the prejudice and ignorance of the writers who wrongly put these words in Jesus' mouth.

SEAN: How do we know what parts of the Bible are merely prejudiced additions?

GLENN: Current scholarship has highly developed literary techniques that enable us to—

SEAN: You mean the current scholarship that is likely to be called antiquated sometime in the future? As far as contemporary scholars' being able to identify the cultural prejudices of the Biblical writers, don't scholars operate with cultural prejudices of their own? If they do, then aren't their conclusions suspect?[1]

GLENN: Scholars can to some degree step outside their own cultural prejudices.

SEAN: Yes they can. So isn't it reasonable to conclude that the Biblical writers were able to step outside theirs?

GLENN: But Jesus would never have taught some of the doctrines ascribed to Him in the Bible.

SEAN: You face a dilemma, Glenn. You want to preserve

the passages of the Bible that you feel demonstrate Jesus' love and tolerance, but you want to reject the Jesus Who warned of Hell and said He was the only way to the Father. For the moment, let's forget the rather dubious literary techniques of modern critics. Answer me this: If you saw your little boy walking down your driveway toward the busy road, what would you do?

GLENN: What any loving parent would do—I would yell out to him to stop.

SEAN: But what if your warning frightened your son?

GLENN: I want it to frighten him. He could get killed if he wandered into the road.

SEAN: What difference does it make to you if your son dies?

GLENN: The answer is obvious. I love him.

SEAN: Yes, I know you do, Glenn. As a matter of fact, you love him enough to warn him even if the warning frightens him. We don't question your love when you warn your son. But wouldn't we be forced to question your love if you knew of the danger and failed to warn him?

GLENN: If the danger really existed, that is.

SEAN: No, if you believed the danger existed. And the Bible clearly teaches that the danger of Hell is real, thus the warning.

GLENN: But my God would never permit anyone to go to Hell.

SEAN: How do you know?

GLENN: Because He isn't cruel.

SEAN: How do you know?

GLENN: Hold on, Sean! I know you don't believe God is cruel.

SEAN: That's right. But I know it because of the testimony of the Bible. How do you know it?

GLENN: Through the Bible. The Bible says God is love.

SEAN: Glenn, you've repeatedly challenged the reliability of the Bible. You've said it contains the error and prejudices of writers who put words into Jesus' mouth—words He never said. Perhaps God is cruel and Jesus was a tyrant, but the Bible erroneously and prejudicially portrays God as loving and Jesus as benevolent. You have no way of knowing. None. Your methodology, your view of the Bible, leaves you unable to say anything about God with any certainty or authority. The bottom line, Glenn, is that your position, applied consistently, leaves you unable to appeal to the Bible for information about this alleged loving God of yours. You state that He exists and that He is too loving to permit anyone to go to Hell. I still want to know, How do you know?

GLENN: How can you believe in a God Who allows people to go to Hell?

SEAN: Glenn, I believe because of the grace of God. I know Him to be loving and merciful because of what He has revealed about Himself in the Bible. You have a problem with Hell. So do I. It's not easy to understand. But you have been less than accurate in your portrayal of Hell. People go there because they have willfully sinned against a holy God Whose justice and righteousness can't just wink at sin the way humans often do. I believe that on the day I step into His presence I will be every bit as overwhelmed by His holiness as Isaiah was in Isaiah 6. In the meantime I trust God's goodness as it is revealed in the Bible, even though I don't fully comprehend His holiness and justice. And I thank God that although I have sinned and deserve Hell, His Son died for me so that by faith in Him I can be delivered from the punishment I deserve and be granted the eternal life I don't deserve.

GLENN: I still don't think what you're saying is reasonable.

SEAN: Glenn, to be perfectly honest with you, the Bible describes your state as being one of unbelief. Your appeal to autonomous reason and your rejection of certain doctrines that you view as antiquated and offensive are not the cause of your unbelief—they are the result of it.

GLENN: So you're saying I'm not a Christian?

SEAN: Glenn, you said a Christian is someone who follows the teachings of Christ. You reject the teachings of Christ as they are presented in the Bible; therefore, you have no reliable source of information, no source of authority to appeal to for information about Jesus Christ. You may continue to embrace the reconstructed Christ of the modern critics and the pastors who follow them, but you do so now knowing that this Christ comes from their own prejudices and wishful thinking. The Bible has a word for such a practice.

GLENN: What is it?

SEAN: Idolatry.

GLENN: Sean, it's a lot easier debating baseball with you than Christianity, but you still haven't persuaded me.

SEAN: It's not my job to argue you into agreement with me, Glenn. What you do with the testimony of the Scriptures is between you and God. I want you to at least see the implications of your position.

GLENN: Okay, but listen to one last thing: John 14:6 still seems too rigid. If it's true, it means that a lot of devoutly religious people will go to Hell. I can't buy that.

SEAN: Glenn, if something is true, it is true whether or not you believe it. But let me use another analogy. Suppose you were a surgeon and someone you love, say your wife, Donna, was dreadfully ill and needed an operation. There are other surgeons around, but only you are capable of correctly performing the needed operation. You tell your wife not to seek out the other surgeons because they can't operate successfully. How credible would the opinion of an outside observer be if he concluded, "Glenn sure is arrogant and intolerant. He should let the other surgeons perform the operation"?

GLENN: That would be foolish. My motivation for claiming that only I could correctly perform the operation would be love for my wife.

SEAN: That's right. And furthermore, it isn't arrogant to simply express what is true. If you're the only one who can do the operation, wouldn't it be morally wrong to withhold that information from your wife?

GLENN: Okay, I think I see where you're going with this.

SEAN: Consider this as well, Glenn. You've often heard it said that explaining God is like a group of blind-folded people describing an elephant. One man touches the trunk and says the elephant is long and powerful like a snake. Another man touches a leg and says the elephant is like a tree. Another man touches a tusk and says the elephant is like a spear. Their descriptions are different, but they are describing the same elephant, and in their own way, each is speaking truth.

GLENN: Actually, I think I've heard that in my church.

SEAN: Then maybe your church is not quite so committed to reason as you believe.

GLENN: What makes you say that?

SEAN: Are you familiar with the law of contradiction?

GLENN: I think so, but let me hear your definition.

SEAN: In its most simple form, the law of contradiction states that A, which can be anything, cannot be both B and non-B at the same time in the same sense. Two contrary things cannot at the same time be identical. If you subscribe to the elephant analogy of religion, you are violating the law of contradiction, which is the foundation of all logic and reason.

GLENN: Even if the analogy does violate the law, and I'm not ready to concede that it does, so what? You quote some obscure, abstract law and act like it is of great importance. In case you haven't noticed, times are changing. Logic and cold rationalism were tools of oppression for the last few centuries. Exalting logic is great if you want to justify totalitarian abuses like slavery, but fortunately we are getting beyond that now. We are free to find our own truth. I'm not going to play your fundamentalist word games.

SEAN: Glenn, without the law of contradiction you would probably be dead right now, and no one could long survive.

GLENN: Is that so?

SEAN: Yes, that's so. When was the last time you ate in a restaurant?

GLENN: Just a couple of days ago.

SEAN: What did you order?

GLENN: Lobster.

SEAN: Ah, my all-time favorite.

GLENN: Mine too.

SEAN: What did your server bring you?

GLENN: I just told you. Lobster.

SEAN: No, you said you ordered lobster. What I'm asking is, What did your server bring you?

GLENN: She served me what I asked for. Lobster.

SEAN: Would you have been upset if she had served you a can of dog food?

GLENN: Of course I would have been upset.

SEAN: Why?

GLENN: What's the matter with you, Sean? If I order lobster, I don't expect to be served dog food.

SEAN: You haven't stopped to think about it, Glenn, but your expectation that you would be served lobster is dependent upon both you and the server's living by the law of contradiction. The law states that for lobster to mean something, there must also be something it doesn't mean. Lobster and dog food are two different things. Demanding that the distinction be maintained is not arrogant or narrow-minded, it is the prerequisite for sanity. Think of what a disaster it would be if we abandoned the law of contradiction. You ask the pharmacist for aspirin, and he gives you cyanide pills. Half the automobile drivers think the red octagonal sign means "stop" and half think it means "accelerate." Real contradictions cannot be harmonized. If they could be, they wouldn't be contradictions.

GLENN: Even if I grant you the point, so what?

SEAN: Now be consistent, Glenn. The only way you can subscribe to the analogy of religion and truth's being like an elephant is by rejecting the law of contradiction. You have also just acknowledged the necessity of the law. Now I ask you, Glenn, what has become of the reason you claim to exercise?

GLENN: But where is the contradiction in saying that all religions lead to God, but each in their own way?

SEAN: They make mutually exclusive claims about their most foundational beliefs. Christianity teaches there is only one God. Hinduism teaches there are thousands of gods. Now logically, Glenn, both may be wrong, but they cannot both be right. To say that both are right violates the fundamental basis of reason, the law of contradiction.

GLENN: But maybe that's okay when we are talking about religion.

SEAN: No, Glenn, I can't let you get away with that. When we began this conversation you told me you could not accept the tenets of historic Christianity, or fundamentalism as you call it, because those fundamentals conflict with what you consider to be reasonable. Now you're telling me reason isn't all its cracked up to be.

GLENN: Reason as you use it.

SEAN: I'm using it reasonably and consistently. How else is it to be used?

[There is silence as Glenn tries to gather his thoughts.]

SEAN: There's something else, Glenn.

GLENN: What?

SEAN: If you now decide to reject reason, it will be only after you have reasoned things out. You would be using reason to decide that reason is unreliable. Thus you are caught in a vicious cycle of self-defeating positions. A verse in Proverbs says, "The fear of the LORD is the beginning of knowledge" (1:7). Glenn, if we don't presuppose the authority and reliability of God's Word from the outset, it is not because we are enlightened but because our minds are darkened. If we want to have true knowledge of God, we must begin by humbly acknowledging the God of the Bible.

Summary of Sean and Glenn

Even though this conversation might seem long and confusing, there are actually just a few key points to which the Christian, Sean, keeps coming back. His cousin Glenn is typical of a great many people, comfortably religious but not true Christians. Glenn has a religion that appeases his conscience without making him take seriously what the Bible has to say about sin and salvation. People such as Glenn want a generic god who doesn't truly challenge human autonomy. They certainly don't want to deal with the specific and authoritative claims of Christ.

Consider the following:

Sean pointed out that Glenn's "relevant" pastor is correct only if her modernistic standards are valid, and Sean cited Colossians 2:8 as rejecting these standards.[2]

Glenn then criticized Sean's rigid adherence to the Bible and the Bible's teaching on Hell and Jesus Christ as the only way to Heaven. Sean pointed out that a person cannot call himself a Christian if he rejects Christ's teaching.

Glenn tried to write off some doctrines as antiquated myths, while he kept those he likes. Sean demonstrated the quicksand of such relativity, for relativity robs us of certainty. The relativist has no logical basis for criticizing the absolutist. The religious relativist cannot make any absolute claims about God's nature, for he has no way of knowing absolutely. The moment he tries to speak in absolute terms, he is being the exact thing he criticizes (dogmatic!).

Sean showed Glenn that as much as Glenn prides himself on being reasonable, he forfeits all claims to reason when he embarks on a relativist path that seeks to reconcile contradictory (mutually exclusive) claims. Glenn then did something interesting. He played the part of the postmodernist and tried to dismiss logic and reason as being irrelevant. It is common for people to drift back and forth between modern and postmodern manners of thought. Both systems have some elements of truth within them, but without an ultimate reference point (God's authoritative Word), they can't be harmonized.

Sean did not allow Glenn to hide behind the irrational or mystical idea that reason doesn't apply to religion because (a) Glenn began the conversation by appealing to reason; he can't discard it now because he doesn't like where it leads; and (b) how can Glenn assert that reason and religion are separate, since Glenn must first use reason in examining his beliefs before he can reach his anti-reason conclusion?

In summary, Sean dealt properly with Glenn by demonstrating that the label "Christian" cannot be worn honestly by someone who rejects the Christ of the Bible. Also, by the use of reason Sean has shown the fallacy of embracing some of the attributes ascribed to God in the Bible while rejecting others. In essence, Sean has shown that a watered-down Christianity that appeals to autonomous reason is neither Christian nor reasonable. Sean understood this fact before he began the conversation with Glenn. By using the ATW approach, Sean helped Glenn see that Glenn's worldview cannot pass the test of internal consistency because it is rooted in error. Remember, every nonbiblical worldview is fatally flawed and that nothing exposes the flaws better than a few carefully crafted questions.

Thinking It Through

1. What do you think is the absolute minimum a person must believe to be a genuine Christian? Upon what Scripture passages would you base your answer?
2. The process of reconciling the doctrine of Hell with a loving God is a challenge over which many Christians struggle, but it is an important question within apologetics. How would you reconcile Hell with a loving God, and what Scripture portions would you use?

3. Those who criticize Hell as being unjust are appealing to some sort of absolute standard against which they judge a holy God. To do this with any consistency, they must subscribe to a worldview within which moral absolutes make sense, or they lose all grounds for accusing God of being unjust. What questions would you ask an unbeliever to have him justify the standards he uses to criticize God? How could you use this justification to demonstrate that unbelievers often unconsciously borrow from the Christian worldview, a worldview they claim to deny?

4. Glenn asked a question that reflects a serious attack against the four Gospels. He claimed that Jesus never spoke many of the words attributed to Him in the Gospels. If Glenn is right and Jesus never said anything like the words in John 14:6 and similar passages, Bible-believing Christianity is in serious trouble. How would you respond to this type of charge?

5. In this encounter Sean made use of the law of contradiction, which is a basic law of logic. Can you find instances of its use (at least indirectly) in the Bible? Do Numbers 23:19, Matthew 5:37, 7:9 and 10, 7:16 and 17, 2 Corinthians 1:17, and James 3:9–12 have any connection with this law of logic?

Notes

1. The conversation between Sean and Glenn is getting close to the dilemma of postmodernist thought. What exactly is postmodernism? Although it can be difficult to define, it has become a major competitor of the Christian worldview in our culture. Appendix D (p. 239) provides a brief overview of postmodernism, and the reader is encouraged to consult it. Also, the fourth encounter ("The Postmodernist," p. 111) portrays a Christian's encounter with a postmodernist. Regarding the present encounter between Sean and Glenn and the issue of Biblical criticism, a valuable resource is Eta Linneman's *Historical Criticism of*

the Bible (see Recommended Reading, page 263). A useful analysis of postmodernism can be found in D. A. Carson's *The Gagging of God.*

2. There may be some confusion over the term "modernist." Historically, religious modernism was a movement that began in the eighteenth century and hit its zenith in the first half of the twentieth century. Modernism rejected many of the historic, supernaturalist aspects of the Bible, while seeking to retain the parts of Christianity it considered compatible with the findings of modern science. This approach became the foundation of theological liberalism. A classic treatment of this development is J. Gresham Machen's *Christianity and Liberalism.* In response to modernism, fundamentalism became a movement with a distinct identity. Although it can be complicated to keep straight, think of religious modernism as a subset within the larger world of philosophical modernism.

Postmodernism represents an overthrow of modernism. Why then do I claim that there are elements of both in the dialogue between Sean and Glenn? For all the differences between the two systems (if you can even call postmodernism a system), they can find common ground in the rejection of historic Christianity. Modernism, which obviously predates postmodernism, was ultimately irrational in spite of its outward commitment to rationalism. Because of its rejection of Christianity, modernism could not ultimately justify its commitment to rationalism and at the same time argue that the universe arose by chance and lacks design or purpose. Viewed this way, both modernism and postmodernism reduce to incoherence, thus an individual such as Glenn can drift back and forth between them.

ENCOUNTER 6

THE SECULAR HUMANIST

UNBELIEVER: Professor Isaac Sagan, a college professor committed to secular humanism. His humanist values are opposed to the Christian worldview, and he is an outspoken critic of Christianity.

BELIEVER: Ron Hauck, a Bible-preaching pastor who understands the contradictions of secular humanism. In this encounter he will use the forum of a popular talk radio program to respond to Professor Sagan's assertions.

HOST: Larry Prince

❖ ❖ ❖

LARRY: We have two guests today. Returning for a second time is Professor Isaac Sagan. Professor Sagan was with us last week. His comments on that show prompted our second guest, Pastor Ron Hauck, to contact us and ask for permission to appear with Professor Sagan for our show today. Professor Sagan enthusiastically agreed, so here we are. Gentlemen, I know that you disagree with each other on many things, so let's approach it like this: Each of you make a brief opening statement so that our audience understands your basic premise, and then we'll let you just go back and forth. If we get bogged down, I'll step in and try to get things back on track. To our friends in the listening audience, I know many people will be calling in to talk to our guests. Please be patient, and we'll try to get as many calls in as we can. But first, let's hear from our guests. Dr. Sagan, why don't you begin.

SAGAN: Thank you, Larry. For thousands of years wars have been fought and people slaughtered in the name of religion, and more specifically in the name of Christianity. In this age of nuclear weapons it is obvious that we must find a more reasonable and intelligent way to view life. Harmful superstitions need to be replaced by an enlightened system of thought and values. It's called humanism. This approach will maximize human freedom and do away with the oppressive tyranny of those motivated by a fanatical commitment to a nonexistent god or gods. I'm not saying all religionists are mad or cruel, but their beliefs are dangerous and ought to be opposed. Humanism is the hope for mankind's future.

LARRY: Thank you, Professor Sagan, for that enlightening introduction. We will now hear from our other guest, Pastor Hauck.

HAUCK: Professor Sagan must not use the word "must"; he needn't use the word "need"; and he ought not use the word "ought." Thank you, Larry.

LARRY: [*recovering from surprise*] Er, ah, I expected you would have more to say on this, Reverend. Professor Sagan has launched a strong attack against your beliefs.

HAUCK: I intend no disrespect to Professor Sagan or to you, Larry. Professor Sagan's attack is worded strongly, but his argument is weak. I have simply responded to its central weakness.

SAGAN: Well now, Larry, I suspect the reason the good Reverend has said so little is because there is so little his side can say in the face of humanism. Christianity should have been embarrassed into silence a long time ago, but I am glad to see that it has finally happened.

HAUCK: Actually, sir, I figured that since your argument is self-defeating, my job is already done. Since my point seems to have escaped both of you, perhaps I should show you the error.

SAGAN: Now that's a laugh. Christianity is a series of errors, contradictions, and superstitions. And yet you are going to lecture me on error?

HAUCK: No, sir. I have no desire to lecture you, although I don't see why a university professor should be opposed to the concept of lecture. Christians do make errors and contradict themselves, and some are even superstitious. But those things come from human flaws in Christians, not the body of truth we call Christianity. I will be happy to address these matters if you are truly interested. However, I would first like to point out the self-defeating nature of your assertions.

SAGAN: Go ahead and try, but I hope you realize that many of the world's most intelligent scholars are humanists.

HAUCK: God has a knack for confounding the wisdom of the world, Professor Sagan. As I listened to you on this program last week, I noticed you repeatedly advocated the concepts put forth in the *Second Humanist Manifesto.* Is that correct?

SAGAN: Yes, the *Manifesto* is something I not only support, but I teach from it in my classes.

HAUCK: I've read the *Manifesto,* Professor Sagan. But it has me stumped. For example, sections five and six are confusing. Larry, would you mind if I read them for the listening audience?

LARRY: Go right ahead.

HAUCK: "Fifth: the preciousness and dignity of the individual person is a central humanist value. Individuals should be encouraged to realize their own creative talents and desires. We reject all religious, ideological, or moral codes that denigrate the individual, suppress freedom, dull intellect, dehumanize personality. We believe in maximum individual autonomy consonant with social responsibility. Although science can account for the causes of behavior, the possibilities of individual freedom of choice exist in human life and should be increased.

"Sixth: In the area of sexuality, we believe that intolerant attitudes, often cultivated by orthodox religions and puritanical cultures, unduly repress sexual conduct. The right to birth control, abortion, and divorce should be recognized. While we do not approve of exploitive, denigrating forms of sexual expression, neither do we wish to prohibit, by law or social sanction, sexual behavior between consenting adults. The many varieties of sexual exploration should not in themselves be considered evil. Without countenancing mindless permissiveness or unbridled promiscuity, a civilized society should be a tolerant one. Short of harming others or compelling them to do likewise, individuals should be permitted to express the sexual proclivities and pursue their life-styles as they desire. We wish to cultivate the development of a responsible attitude toward sexuality, in which humans are not exploited as sexual objects, and in which intimacy, sensitivity, respect, and honesty in interpersonal relations are encouraged. Moral education for children and adults is an important way of developing awareness and sexual maturity."[1]

My basic question is this: why?

SAGAN: Why what?

HAUCK: Why do you assert these things rather than their opposites? And why do you use imperatives? Let's go through these assertions I've just read out of the *Humanist Manifesto*. "The preciousness and dignity of the individual person is a humanist value." Why should this matter? And just because it matters to you, why should it matter to me or to Joseph Stalin? "We reject all religious, ideological, or moral codes that denigrate the individual, suppress freedom, dull intellect, dehumanize personality." Why?

And just because it matters to you, why should it matter to me? What is wrong with my using my freedom to suppress your freedom?

SAGAN: The answer to your questions is found in the next statement of the *Manifesto*. "We believe in maximum individual autonomy consonant with social responsibility." You can't use your freedom to suppress someone else's freedom because it is socially irresponsible.

HAUCK: But why should I subscribe to your definition of social responsibility? What happens to the people who don't adhere to the definition of social responsibility as proclaimed by "enlightened humanists"? What if a large segment of the population decides that the socially responsible thing to do is to imprison all humanists? Why would that be wrong?

SAGAN: That is the difference between you and me, Reverend Hauck, and I'm glad people have heard it come out of your mouth. You would imprison people who disagree with you, and the church has done exactly that throughout history. Humanists would approach the area of disagreement by seeking to educate the ignorant, not kill them.

LARRY: I'm afraid he's got you there, Reverend. What can you possibly say to the professor now?

HAUCK: You haven't answered my basic question of why. You seem to be content to use questionable historical analogies that cloud over the issue of why. Since I fear that at this rate we will not get to examine the flawed logic of humanism, let me take a minute to respond to your charges. There are several blemishes one can find in church history, Professor Sagan, although I wish you were as quick to notice the countless wonderful deeds of Christianity such as hospitals built, works of self-sacrifice and charity, and the establishment of orphanages, shelters, universities, and many other things too numerous to mention. Wherever we find a blemish, it is because of Christians deviating from the standards of Biblical Christianity. The problem, therefore, is not with the Christian faith; it is with the failure of mortal men and women to consistently practice it. I could sit here all day and point out flawed humanists just as readily as you can point out flawed Christians. It seems to me that if we want to be intellectually honest and serious, we will focus on the systems themselves and see if they are at fault for the behavior of their practitioners. Besides that, Professor Sagan, the Bible is more critical of hypocrisy than you are. In Matthew 7:22 and 23 Jesus said that many who call themselves Christians are not the genuine item. Events like the Spanish Inquisition are not the result of Christians practicing Biblical Christianity. Such actions violate what the Bible says. Now if your use of church history is anything more than a smokescreen, I suggest we schedule a separate program for that purpose, and I will gladly discuss it with you. History has much to teach us about the dangers of rejecting the Bible. Would that be okay with you, Larry?

LARRY: I think we're getting sidetracked, gentlemen. Reverend Hauck, you were raising questions about the *Manifesto*. Remind us of what you were saying, and then we'll let Professor Sagan answer you.

HAUCK: I was pointing out that the *Manifesto* makes numerous assertions about the way things ought to be. What I want to know is why the rest of us should believe that those particular things are true. Aren't they just the arbitrary opinions of the humanists? For example, the *Manifesto* states that Christianity unduly represses sexual conduct and that such intolerance is intolerable. It tells us that the many varieties of sexual exploration should not in themselves be considered evil. It then turns around and places some restrictions on human sexuality such as exploitation, denigration, mindless permissiveness, unbridled promiscuity, and nonconsensual sex. But why would it be wrong for a man to explore his sexuality by exploiting women? Why is it wrong to rape children? Because it is nonconsensual? Why should that matter? The *Manifesto* says that "short of harming others or compelling them to do likewise, individuals should be permitted to express their sexual proclivities and pursue their lifestyles as they desire." But why should a man have to draw his line where Dr. Sagan says? What reason does Dr. Sagan give for saying we should stop short of harming others? And as far as the *Manifesto*'s encouraging relationships that are intimate, sensitive, respectful, and honest, why is that better than relationships that are distant, insensitive, disrespectful, and deceitful? The bottom line to all this, Dr. Sagan, is that there are many assertions made in the *Humanist Manifesto*. I simply want to know why these assertions should be seen as desirable and true.

LARRY: Despite Reverend Hauck's rather lengthy sermon, I think we were able to follow it. I must say that the answers to his questions are so obvious that I hate to waste time having Dr. Sagan answer them. Dr. Sagan, please address Reverend Hauck's questions, and then we'll move onto something more substantive.

SAGAN: Certainly. Some of our listeners might think that Reverend Hauck is clever, but his questions are rather foolish. I'll answer by using two terms: compassion and wisdom. As a humanist I oppose exploitation because it lacks compassion. I acknowledge the preciousness and dignity of the individual for the same reason, and I will never apologize for being compassionate.

LARRY: Amen!

SAGAN: Wisdom also tells us that the humanist values are necessary for the survival of humanity, not to mention progress. Some have called this "enlightened self-interest." In other words, since I don't want to be raped or robbed, it is wise for me to refrain from those activities myself. We don't use nuclear weapons against another nation because we don't want that nation using such weapons against us. Frankly, I would have to question the intelligence of any person who fails to see the wisdom of these values. Reject these values and you condemn the human race to destruction.

LARRY: I was right; the answers are obvious. Thank you, Dr. Sagan. Comments, Reverend Hauck?

HAUCK: No, another question. My question is, so what? So what if you're compassionate? So what if you preserve the existence of humanity? Why does it matter? If I choose cruelty over compassion or extermination over existence, why does it really matter?

SAGAN: Larry, this is ridiculous. This man isn't even trying to be reasonable.

HAUCK: No Larry, it is my commitment to reason that compels me to ask these questions. It is my commitment to reason that prompts me to examine the things that Dr. Sagan merely assumes by faith. I share some of Dr. Sagan's values, although I reject others. I oppose rape, exploitation, and the denial of the value of each individual, but my reasons for holding these values are reasonable. Dr. Sagan's are not.

SAGAN: I teach at one of the finest universities in America, and we're supposed to listen to a superstitious preacher?

HAUCK: Dr. Sagan, I draw my values from something greater than myself—an infinite Creator God Who has revealed these values to us, for we are His creatures, the creatures to whom He granted life. These things are true because the sovereign Creator reveals them as such. Individuals have value because they are created in the image of God. If we do not derive our values from something greater than ourselves, then our values are merely something we have invented. This makes them arbitrary and subjective, no matter how passionately we believe them. What this means is that in your worldview the three of us might all despise Adolf Hitler's value system, but we cannot judge or condemn it. Hitler's system is not our personal preference, but it is not wrong in the absolute sense. This is why I have spent most of my allotted time on the program asking Dr. Sagan the same question over and over: why?

SAGAN: None of what you have said proves that God exists. You believe what you do because of faith, so why do you criticize me for having faith in the value of my assertions? Not only that, Reverend Hauck, I find no evidence for this so-called Creator of yours.

HAUCK: I have not yet attempted to prove to you that God exists. I do not deny that my belief in Him includes an element of faith, but I am convinced that my faith is more reasonable than your faith, Dr. Sagan. I presuppose the truthfulness of the Bible. It is my starting point, and my values are a logical outgrowth of my core beliefs or worldview. Yours are not. My worldview can account for moral imperatives; yours cannot. Consider these words from the *Humanist Manifesto:*

"But we can discover no divine purpose or providence for the human species. While there is much that we do not know, humans are responsible for what we are or will become. No deity will save us; we must save ourselves. Promises of immortal salvation or fear of eternal damnation are both illusory and harmful. They distract humans from present concerns, from self-actualization, and from rectifying social injustices. Modern science discredits such historic concepts as the 'ghost in the machine' and the 'separable soul.' Rather, science affirms that the human species is an emergence from natural evolutionary forces. As far as we know, the total personality is a function of the biological organism transacting in a social and cultural context. There is no credible evidence that life survives the death of the body."

Dr. Sagan, this document asserts that life arose by chance, not purpose. It insists that this mortal life is all there is; there is no existence beyond the grave. If these things are true, then your entire value system is suspect. What if someone with your beliefs about God and eternity has a totally different response? Why are your values better than those of Aldous Huxley?

LARRY: And what exactly did Huxley say?

HAUCK: Huxley said, "I had motives for not wanting the world to have a meaning; consequently I assumed that it had none, and was able without any difficulty to find satisfying reasons for this assumption. The philosopher who finds no meaning in the world is not concerned exclusively with a problem in pure metaphysics, he is also concerned to prove that there is no valid reason why he personally should not do as he wants to do, or why his friends should not seize political power and govern in the way that they find most advantageous to themselves. . . . For myself, the philosophy of meaninglessness was essentially an instrument of liberation, sexual and political."[2]

Dr. Sagan, I would like to ask you one more time. Why is your way better than Huxley's?

SAGAN: Do you mean to say that mine isn't better?

HAUCK: I want to know what standard you use to determine which is better. Without a God Who reveals what is better, I don't see how you have any basis other than your own subjective opinion, an opinion with which Aldous Huxley couldn't be bothered. Actually Huxley might have been interested in your opinion because it makes you easier to conquer. I don't like Huxley's values, but without an authority greater than finite humans we are reduced to one man's opinion versus another man's, and the man with the most power, if he's willing to use it, will get his way. And if that's Huxley and his friends, then where does that leave us?

SAGAN: Well, Reverend Hauck, I have a serious problem with your appeal to a higher authority. What right do you have to speak for this so-called God? Why you, and not David Koresh or Osama bin Laden?

HAUCK: That's a valid question, Dr. Sagan, but before I answer it, I want you to know that until you can surmount my critique of your ethical system, you must either abandon your moral values or base them upon something else. And, Dr. Sagan, I don't think you will abandon your moral values. I think you will continue to believe that the rape of children is wrong. I think that in your heart you will continue to believe that subjecting an entire race of people to torture and genocide in the name of ethnic cleansing is not just socially disruptive, it is really wrong, it is genuinely evil. Dr. Sagan, this moral sense of yours is evidence that in spite of your denials, you know God exists and that in spite of your rebellion against Him, you can't escape the fact that you bear the image of God. My prayer for you is that you will acknowledge the God Who has

given you the moral conscience you have displayed
here tonight and place your faith in Jesus Christ. As
far as who has the right to speak for God, I have my
Bible here with me—

LARRY: Gentlemen, I'm afraid that's all the time we have.
I want to thank both of you for a most interesting
time. To the many listeners who have called, you
will have to save your calls for our next program.

Summary of Pastor Hauck and Dr. Sagan

Pastor Hauck was correct when he chose to ask Professor Sagan to defend his use of imperatives. By "imperatives" we mean
the *Manifesto*'s use of words such as "must" and "ought." If there
is no transcendent God Who issues commandments, if there is no
ultimate design or purpose to the universe, then there is no valid
basis for using words such as "must." One can have Professor Sagan's beliefs about God and the universe and quite logically reject
all acts of kindness and compassion. If Professor Sagan responds
by asserting that it is in our best interest to be kind to others, we
will again ask why we must define self-interest the same way he
does. For example, we could take a position like this one: I will
die someday, and there is no judgment to follow. I would rather
live life wildly and die violently as a young man than to be gentle
and compassionate and die as an old man. In the grand scheme
of the universe—which really has no grand design—my life and
yours do not matter. Sagan's values do not matter. I hope he continues to live by them though, because his values will make him
that much more vulnerable to those of us who choose to rob and
kill.

Professor Sagan had no legitimate answer to this scenario, so
he chose to attack church history and raise the question of "who
speaks for God." The Christian needs to be ready to respond to
these tactics.

Professor Sagan's philosophy of ethics, seen in this encounter, is anything but fictional. A real-life example can be found in the writings of renowned atheistic philosopher Kai Neilsen. Neilsen has written extensively to refute the Christian proposition that meaningful ethics without God is impossible. Neilsen's views can be examined by reading the transcripts of a debate in which he participated on March 24, 1988, at the University of Mississippi. His opponent was Christian philosopher J. P. Moreland. (See J. P. Moreland and Kai Nielsen, *Does God Exist? The Great Debate* [Nashville: Thomas Nelson Publishers, 1990].) Both men delivered lectures before the debate, and Nielsen used the opportunity to claim that ethics without God could rely on the "fair adjudication" of a society. To Nielsen's assertions we once again ask why. If I choose anarchy over fair adjudication, why is my choice less valid? By what standard can Nielsen reject my desire for anarchy? I might not be in the majority, but appealing to the majority can be dangerous! Society will not last with widespread anarchy, but again we ask, Why do I have to accept your opinion that we should preserve society?

The most clever response that a non-Christian can use is this one: The desire to preserve the human species is a genetic trait that is a part of how we have evolved. Humanistic values are the tool we use to do what comes naturally.

A good response to this line of thinking can be found in the third encounter ("The Evolutionist," p. 97). But we will once again raise the question, Why does it matter? According to evolutionists, millions of species have come and gone. If I choose to reject my evolutionary programming and seek to obliterate humanity by killing as many people as I can, have I done something truly immoral? Maybe my rejection of my evolutionary programming is actually the next step in human evolution.

Finally, please note that near the end of the encounter Pastor Hauck articulated the presuppositionalist view of morality. If God is not presupposed as the ground of morality, no system of ethics can be devised that will be anything but arbitrary and relative. And any system that is arbitrary and relative cannot truly justify the claim that raping children is wrong. When seen in this light, such a system is difficult for even the staunchest skeptic to accept.

Thinking It Through

1. Dr. Sagan used the blemishes found throughout church history to attack Reverend Hauck's faith. How would you handle such a tactic?

2. Matthew 7:21-23, Galatians 2:11-14, and 1 John 1:8—2:2 can be helpful for explaining why there are blemishes in church history. In what ways do these and similar passages not only explain the blemishes, but actually strengthen the truth claims of Christianity?

3. In what way did Reverend Hauck apply Proverbs 26:4 and 5 to this encounter?

4. In what way did Dr. Sagan unwittingly reflect Proverbs 2:14 and 15?

5. Dr. Sagan mentioned Osama bin Laden and David Koresh and then asked an important, difficult question, Who speaks for God? It deserves a careful answer. When you share the gospel of Jesus Christ, you are in a sense speaking for God. Please read Matthew 28:18-20, Acts 1:8, and 2 Corinthians 5:16-20. What gives a Christian the right to speak for God? What are some potential mistakes Christians might make when speaking for God?

Notes

1. The excerpts used in this encounter come from the *Humanist Manifesto* of 1973. It was signed by over two hundred humanists, many

of them active in academic circles. The original *Humanist Manifesto* was drafted in 1933 and spoke in glowing terms of the future of humanism. The darkness of World War II, the Holocaust, and the Stalin regime dampened some of the optimism found in the 1933 version, thus the *Second Manifesto* of 1973. Since then, another *Manifesto* came out in 2000. I chose to use the excerpts from 1973 because they provide useful illustrations. It is my contention that the newest version (and all future versions that reflect humanist presuppositions) contain the same fundamental weaknesses addressed in this encounter.

2. Aldous Huxley, *Ends and Means* (New York: Harper, 1937), n.p.

THE VALUES CLARIFIER

UNBELIEVER: Ms. Smith, teacher. Ms. Smith is a thirty-two-year-old public-school teacher and considers herself to be open minded and progressive. She is currently teaching English to high school juniors.

BELIEVER: Courtney, student. Courtney is sixteen years old and has been reared in a solid Christian home. Courtney's parents have taught her to evaluate all ideas and teachings in light of the Bible. This training will serve her well, for today she will be asked to participate in a classroom exercise that occurs in countless classrooms around the country every year.

❖ ❖ ❖

Ms. SMITH: Class, put away your books. Today we are going

to do something different, something I think you will really enjoy. It is going to require that you use your imagination and engage in clear thinking. On the chalkboard you see brief descriptions of fifteen people. Who are they? Well, along with you, they are the only survivors of a terrible disaster at sea. They were passengers on an ocean liner that sank due to a sudden and violent explosion. You were the captain of that ship, and now the sixteen of you are adrift in a small lifeboat. As the captain, you are in command. Now here's the problem: The ship sank so quickly that there was not time to send out a distress call. Therefore, no one knows of the accident, so no rescue effort is in the works. By the time anyone realizes something is wrong, they will have no idea where to conduct the search. This means that your little lifeboat may be left on the open sea for many days, if not weeks. You have little food and water, and the lifeboat is made to hold only eight people, so there is a strong likelihood that it will capsize or sink with sixteen people. It is clear to you that under these circumstances no one will survive more than a couple of days. With deep remorse you realize that the only hope of anyone surviving is to eliminate some of the passengers. The food and water could then be made to last longer, and the lifeboat would be more seaworthy if there were eight people rather than sixteen. If you don't take drastic measures, all sixteen people will be dead within days. As captain, you must choose eight people who will be put overboard. You don't want to do this, but you know that they will die anyway. At least now some might survive.

Now look at the descriptions of the fifteen passengers on the chalkboard. I will read them off one at a time, and after each one we will vote by a show of hands. I want to hear your reasons for your vote, whether it be yes or no. As the captain you must remain on the lifeboat because you are the only one with any knowledge of survival on the open sea. Are we ready? Let's begin. [*Courtney raises her hand.*]

MS. SMITH: Yes, Courtney?

COURTNEY: Why are we doing this, Ms. Smith?

MS. SMITH: Courtney, this is a helpful exercise. It helps to teach critical thinking and to examine our values.

COURTNEY: This is wrong, Ms. Smith, and I don't think you should ask us to do this.

MS. SMITH: [*trying not to lose her temper*] We do this every year, Courtney, and not only is it popular with our students, it is a respected teaching tool. If you insist on complaining about this exercise, I will excuse you to the library.

COURTNEY: Ms. Smith, I'm not trying to be disruptive, but this lesson doesn't make sense.

MS. SMITH: [*with a knowing smile*] Oh, I see your problem now, Courtney. You misunderstand what we are doing. This lifeboat situation is obviously not normal; it is a special situation, and you're looking at it the wrong way. You're not being asked to kill eight people; you're being asked to save eight people! If you don't make these hard choices, all sixteen will die. At least this way some will survive, and I think we can all agree that eight survivors are better than no survivors and eight deaths are not as bad as sixteen deaths.

COURTNEY: But on what are we supposed to base our choices? Look at the first two people. Number one is a seventy-four-year-old retired widower. Number two is a thirty-one-year-old female scientist. How am I supposed to choose between them?

MS. SMITH: That's the point of the whole exercise, Courtney. You have to make a difficult judgment. It may not be easy, but that's life in the real world.

COURTNEY: Well, then, why not kill everyone?

MS. SMITH: [*somewhat flabbergasted*] That's ridiculous, Courtney. There's no need to kill everyone.

COURTNEY: But I want to.

MS. SMITH: Courtney, I'm shocked at you. You can't just kill people because you want to.

COURTNEY: Why not?

MS. SMITH: It's wrong, and you know it.

COURTNEY: Why is it wrong? You have already told me I should kill eight people. I'm just going a little further than you.

MS. SMITH: I'm not doing it because I want to, but because it needs to be done. It's the only chance of anyone surviving.

COURTNEY: What if I don't want anyone to survive?

MS. SMITH: [*raising her voice*] I don't know what you're up to, Courtney, but I don't appreciate it. We're trying to do something useful and important.

COURTNEY: So am I, Ms. Smith. I'm doing exactly what you said. I'm thinking critically. You said it's permissible to choose to kill certain people, so that is what I am doing. Now you're saying I'm wrong for killing more people than you are killing. Can you give me a sound reason for your opinion?

MS. SMITH: There is value to human life, Courtney. We demonstrate that value by making difficult choices so that some might survive.

COURTNEY: So human life is valuable? Can you tell me why? And if it is valuable, why kill eight people? Because eight dead is better than sixteen? Isn't it just as reasonable to say that because life is valuable we should not cheapen it by applying arbitrary judgments to justify killing eight people? On the other hand, if arbitrary judgments are acceptable, why can't I arbitrarily judge that I would rather kill all fifteen passengers than just eight? [*She pauses to let this sink in, then continues.*] Ms. Smith, you said the purpose of this exercise is to encourage critical thinking and the examination of values. I don't need such an exercise. I know what my values are, and I know why I believe them. The way you've presented this exercise ignores critical thinking, and it clouds values. It doesn't clarify them.

MS. SMITH: You don't have a problem killing fifteen people?

COURTNEY: Why does that bother you? You're ready to kill eight.

MS. SMITH: So that eight more can survive.

COURTNEY: And that's good?

MS. SMITH: Eight survivors rather than none? Yes, that is good!

COURTNEY: Are you absolutely sure about that?

MS. SMITH: Yes I'm sure. Now please make your point so that the class can continue.

COURTNEY: The point, Ms. Smith, is that you are illogical, and you are not promoting critical thinking but confused thinking. This exercise calls for relativism, and yet when I take the liberty to carry it further than you want, you start appealing to absolutes. That is a contradiction. To make things worse, you can't justify your absolutes. This seems to be tyranny, not open-mindedness. You have opened what my dad calls a logical can of worms. You accept the legitimacy of killing eight people who are not as valuable as the rest. You have no absolute standards, you rely on your own reason, and you ask us to do the same. A verse in the Bible says, "There is a way that seems right to a man, but its end is the way of death." If you want to talk about the real world, Ms. Smith, what would you say if I told you I have a real gun in my desk and I want to use it to shoot you because a substitute teacher will give me a higher grade? Would you still be sure you want to live in a relativistic world?

Summary of Courtney and Ms. Smith

Not too many teenagers think like Courtney because not too many adults think like Courtney. She is both logical and Biblical, and it is important for all Christians to be taught to think in these terms. (This training can be done if less time is spent with the television.) Courtney was prepared to dissect Ms. Smith's thinking, while Ms. Smith was not truly prepared to defend it. Of course, she thought she was, as is evidenced in her appeal to the desirability of eight survivors rather than none. But Courtney's parents have taught her well; she easily spotted the error in Ms. Smith's thinking. Did you?

Given more time Courtney would have stated her reliance upon God's absolute standards, standards that reveal Ms. Smith's exercise to be arbitrary, fallible, and wicked. Her first goal, however, was to show that Ms. Smith's worldview is flawed because relativism cannot be used consistently unless one is willing to permit nihilism or anarchy. Courtney was alluding to this prospect by stating her "desire" to kill all fifteen rather than to stop at eight.

Courtney's first question, which was a problem for Ms. Smith, was the question of criteria for choosing those who would be sacrificed. Ms. Smith did not want to volunteer the criteria because she wanted the students to develop and use their own criteria. Relativism (the lack of universal moral absolutes) is clearly implied in Ms. Smith's methodology. To make a point, Courtney took the relativism condoned by Ms. Smith and turned it against her. Courtney decided that her approach would be to kill everyone.

Ms. Smith rejected this approach, saying that such a course of action would be wrong. Ms. Smith has fallen into the trap that every moral relativist who stops short of anarchy falls into. She drew a moral line and expected Courtney to abide by it. She contradicted herself by initially extolling relativism and then by appealing to an absolute standard when the relativism went too far for her taste.

Ms. Smith had to admit that there is value to human life; thus killing all fifteen when some could possibly survive is wrong. Courtney then asked the question, Why is human life valuable? If Ms. Smith answered in a convincing way and established the value of life, she would then be in the position of having to justify killing eight people whose lives were of value. If only some lives are valuable (this may be an underlying assumption in tests such as these), then the question again is, why? By what standard is value determined? If it is an absolute standard, what is it, and where does it come from? Since relativists don't like to acknowledge universal moral absolutes, Ms. Smith is shown to be totally arbitrary and subjective and is left with no reliable criteria for rejecting Courtney's different criteria.

Ms. Smith has two choices. She must grant Courtney the right to kill all fifteen as a morally neutral act. If she is not willing to grant this permission, what is her justification for finding Courtney's choice to be immoral? It can be immoral only if there really are universal moral absolutes that are true at all times. Yet to admit the existence of moral absolutes not only undermines the moral relativism of the lifeboat, it gets dangerously close to acknowledging an authoritative God. If Ms. Smith were to say that killing eight is the lesser of two evils (the greater evil being all sixteen dying of thirst) and that the survival of some is still better than the survival of none, she needs to be asked yet again: Why? What standard are you appealing to? Where does it come from, and why is it universal? The Christian can answer these questions consistently; the non-Christian cannot.

The Christian response is not easy, but it is consistent and necessary. God is sovereign. He knows about the lifeboat and the dangers of the sea. He forbids the premeditated killing of people in the name of "value judgment." He is to be obeyed even if it means death, for this complete obedience is honoring to Him. Sinful men resent God's supremacy, so they take matters into their own hands and are quick to reject God's Word. Is this preferable to dying in a lifeboat because we refuse to throw anyone overboard? No. To honor God's Word is mankind's highest duty, even though it may cost them their lives.

Sadly, many Christians might also be persuaded that the

survival of eight is more important than God's Word, even if it means killing eight others. Courtney's use of reason (which is in submission to the authority of Scripture) has demonstrated the far darker consequences for a society that embraces relativism.

On a personal note, I participated in an exercise virtually identical to this one when I was in the seventh grade. All these years later I look back on it with some justifiable resentment. My classmates and I enjoyed the exercise because it was a novel departure from the routine of our English class. That we were being led down the path of moral relativism was not explained to us. The folly of this exercise was not explained. Actually, I suspect that the teacher was thrilled with the concept of moral relativism.

Over the years I have tried this exercise on various church groups when teaching apologetics. My goal is to see how many Christians immediately recognize the anti-Biblical spirit of the exercise. Many Christians take the bait and participate in the exercise without understanding its erroneous nature. Unlike my seventh grade English teacher, I make sure no one is left with the mistaken impression that moral relativism is an acceptable basis for ethics and morality. Invariably, several of the people on whom I have tried this exercise testify that they had similar lessons in school. Sadly, their experiences were similar to mine in that their teachers were seldom, if ever, critical of moral relativism.

Thinking It Through

1. Much of this encounter addresses the issue of the value of life. What is the Biblical basis for the value of life?

2. How would you respond to someone who advocates euthanasia? Along with Scriptural considerations, what are some practical dangers of accepting euthanasia as a morally acceptable practice? Can you think of a scenario where ATW could be a useful tool for dialoguing with someone who supports "mercy killing"?

3. Critics of the Bible often point out that 1 Samuel 15:2 and
   3 portray God as having commanded the extermination of
   the Amalekites. This command seems to contradict the sixth
   commandment: "Thou shalt not kill" (Exod. 20:13, KJV).
   How would you respond to the charge of inconsistency?

4. In the account recorded in Joshua 2:2–6, Rahab lied when
   questioned about the Israelite spies, and then Hebrew 11:31
   commends her for her faith. Her action and this commenda-
   tion seem to contradict the ninth commandment: "Thou shalt
   not bear false witness" (Exod. 20:16, KJV). Isn't this the moral relativism that this encounter seeks to refute? If not, what
   is the difference?

THE PLURALIST

UNBELIEVER: Amy, a twenty-six-year-old legislative aide living in Washington, D.C. Amy is a religious pluralist, which means she believes that all religions are basically of equal value. She believes it is wrong to promote one religious system if it means rejecting others. In the immediate aftermath of the terror attacks of September 11, 2001, there were several interfaith rallies around America. The rallies were inspirational to those who believe unity is a higher good than recognizing the logical contradictions that exist among different religions. Pluralists are often indignant with Bible-practicing Christians, who insist on preaching Christ as the only way. In the years following September 11, 2001, the pressure on Christians to embrace pluralism has grown.

BELIEVER: Twenty-six-year-old Joy also works in Washington D.C. Joy is going to be pressured to offer a "pinch of incense" at the altar of religious pluralism. In the early years of Christianity (prior to AD 313), Christians were often accused of being atheists or of being disloyal to the Roman Empire because they would not worship Roman gods or offer a pinch of incense to the image of the Emperor. The pinch of incense was to be accompanied by the words "Caesar is Lord." Rome did not require Christians to forsake Christ, just to acknowledge their loyalty to the Emperor. Christians were not disloyal, but they saw that it would be an act of idolatry to offer incense to Caesar and that doing so would be a denial of Christ. This is what the Roman Empire could not understand or tolerate—Christianity's stubborn refusal to practice pluralism.

AMY: I can't believe you're not going to the community interfaith meeting. You are one of the most religious people I know.

JOY: I knew you would be expecting me to go. Why do you think I should be there?

AMY: If there was ever a time when people of different faiths should come together, it should be now. The thought of religious wars is terrifying. One would hope that wars like that would be a thing of the past. The most important thing we can do is get together, understand, and tolerate each other, and to join each other in praying for worldwide peace and healing.

JOY: Who will be leading the meeting?

AMY: Oh, it's wonderful what a large cross-section of people will be there. I don't know their names, but

I know there will be a Jewish rabbi, a Roman Catholic cardinal, an Episcopalian bishop, an Islamic imam, a Buddhist monk, a Hindu priest, and representatives of other religions too.

JOY: Sounds like a diverse group.

AMY: It is diverse, and that's what is so exciting. On top of that, several prominent entertainers will be there. And word is that both Republican and Democratic leaders will attend and that they'll actually sit together.

JOY: Amy, I'm glad that in America we have freedom of conscience and that such a diverse group of people can gather in a peaceful assembly. I'm grateful they believe citizens need to share a concern for our nation. And while I appreciate your invitation, I think I'll pass.

AMY: Wait a minute, Joy. I think I know why you don't want to go. You're unwilling to pray with people of other religions, aren't you?

JOY: I'll say this as gently as I can, Amy. My desire is to pray *for* them, but I would be a hypocrite if I prayed *with* them.

AMY: Pray *for* them? Are you saying God hears your prayers but not theirs? Is that why you won't pray with them?

JOY: If I give you an honest answer, will you be willing to discuss it with me?

AMY: You bet I'll discuss it with you. I already know your answer, and I think it is outrageous. How can you possibly say such a mean, bigoted thing?

JOY: Hold on Amy, let me give you an answer, and then we can critique it together. Agreed?

AMY: Okay, go ahead.

JOY: I believe in respecting other people, because in God's eyes they have value. But there is only one way to God, and it is through Jesus Christ. People choose to take other paths, but they don't lead to God, no matter what people think. Does God hear the prayer of non-Christians? Well of course He does. He hears everything that everyone says, whether they're praying to a tree or ordering a cheeseburger at the drive-thru. But no one can enlist God or seek Him as an ally unless they seek Him through His Son, Jesus. For me to believe this and then view the prayers of a Muslim, a Hindu, and a Christian as being equally valid would be hypocritical. My desire is to share the message of Jesus Christ with my Muslim and Hindu neighbors, and to pray that they will trust Him as their personal Savior.

AMY: [*shocked and angered*] How can you say such a terrible thing?

JOY: I said something terrible?

AMY: Yes.

JOY: I stated my belief, and I think it is true. Is that so terrible?

AMY: The arrogance of your belief is monumental. You think you have an exclusive claim on God, and you think everyone who disagrees with you is going to Hell.

JOY: Is that wrong?

AMY: Yes!

JOY: Why is it wrong?

AMY: Because no one has a right to say someone else's religion is wrong.

JOY: How do you know?

AMY: How do I know what?

JOY: How do you know no one has the right to say someone else's religion is wrong?

AMY: Well, you do have the right politically; you're not going to be arrested for being judgmental. But it's not all right to say it, if you know what I mean.

JOY: I think what you're saying is that I am doing something morally wrong when I criticize someone else's religion and refrain from praying with them.

AMY: Yes, that's it. Just look at where religious bigotry and intolerance have brought us today. And I'm not just talking about terrorism. I'm talking about the hatred being spewed out by fundamentalist Christians too.

JOY: I have a question for you, Amy. How is it that you can criticize my religious beliefs, beliefs that you either have misunderstood or have misrepresented, when you have just finished saying that criticizing someone else's religion is unacceptable?

AMY: I respect and tolerate everyone's religious beliefs. The only exception to that is when it becomes too extreme. The vast majority of Muslims are peaceful. The small minority of extremists are the problem. The same holds true for Christianity.

JOY: Who draws the line?

AMY: What do you mean?

JOY: What special insight do you have, Amy, that gives you the ability to say what's extreme and what isn't? It sounds like you're anxious to justify your brand of intolerance, but you deny me that same privilege.

AMY: How dare you say I'm intolerant.

JOY: I'm not insulting you, Amy. I'm just pointing out that you believe there are at least some things that should not be tolerated. You are against the torture of babies and the raping of women, and you would not be open to arguments that attempted to justify those actions. I'm only asking what things you find intolerable and how you justify your conclusions. By what authority do you make those judgments?

AMY: Some things are just self-evident. If a religion promotes killing abortion providers or terrorizing gays, if it embraces mindless dogmatism or preaches hatred against people of other religions, then it should be criticized. I guess to that degree you could say that there are some things I don't tolerate, but I don't know how any reasonable person could see it any other way.

JOY: Do you know of such a religion?

AMY: I just described militant Christianity.

JOY: That's odd, Amy, because I am a Christian and I take the Bible seriously. I don't know of any Biblically literate Christians who fit your description. There may be some crackpots who twist the

Scriptures, but if you would visit my church with me next Sunday, I think you would see how mis-informed your opinion is. Can you cite a passage of New Testament Scripture that advocates terrorizing gays or teaches hatred of non-Christians?

AMY: If I attend your church, I'm sure I'll hear that unless I become a Christian I'll go to Hell.

JOY: Quite possibly you would hear that, Amy. But let me ask you a question. We both believe God exists. We disagree over how God can be approached. I advocate a narrow and exclusive way, one which says Jesus Christ is the only way. You think that there are many ways, and you are offended by what you consider to be intolerance and bigotry on my part.

AMY: Yes, that's about right. Now what's your question?

JOY: Isn't God allowed to state the terms by which He can be approached? Doesn't He have the right to choose what He accepts and what He rejects? I mean, It's one thing to say I don't have the right to be dogmatic, but would you deny God that right?

AMY: I believe God has that right, but I can't believe He could be as intolerant and narrow-minded as you are.[1]

JOY: Are you sure about that?

AMY: Yes.

JOY: So you are willing to make dogmatic statements about the nature of God and that's fine; but if I do it, you won't tolerate it. Amy, don't you see that every-thing you condemn in me you practice yourself?

AMY: That's not true. My whole approach to religion is built on tolerance.

JOY: Amy, I know you believe that, but can I just remind you of some of the things you have said in the last few minutes? At various points you have accused me of being mean, bigoted, intolerant, and outrageous. All of this criticism is your response to my belief that God has the right to choose how He is to be approached. I believe God has revealed that the only way is through Jesus Christ. Rather than getting mad at God for limiting my options, I have chosen to take Him at His Word. I don't believe that I or anyone else has the right to dictate to God. How does that make me mean or intolerant?

AMY: But I don't believe God limits how we can approach Him. As long as we are sincere and respectful of others who choose a different path, then God will accept us.

JOY: Did He tell you that?

AMY: What do you mean?

JOY: Well, you are making a claim about what God is like and how He thinks. You are so sure of your knowledge that you use it as a basis for criticizing me in rather strong terms. I also make claims about God. Our claims vastly differ from one another's, so they can't both be right. So tell me, Amy, did God appear to you and reveal this information, or did you come across it some other way? Could you tell me who or what your source is and how you know it's reliable?

AMY: I don't think its worth discussing because I'm sure

we don't agree. But I'm certainly not going to resort to thumping the Bible.

JOY: Do you reject the Bible as being a trustworthy record of God's revelation to mankind?

AMY: Other religions make similar claims for their sacred writings, so where does it get us?

JOY: Well, at least the Bible provides a meaningful starting point for investigating true claims about God and how He is to be approached. Amy, would it be okay if I show you what the Bible says about the way to God and why I believe the Bible can be trusted? I would be more than willing to consider any reasons you have for what you believe.

AMY: I'll give you a few minutes, but I need to get going to the interfaith meeting.

JOY: Thanks Amy. Let's begin by considering John 14:6 and what would be reasonable grounds for believing those words. . . .

Summary of Joy and Amy

It took several questions, but Joy was able to bring the discussion to a point where meaningful investigation of opposing views could take place. If Amy is willing to pursue the discussion, then Joy and Amy can examine not only the truth claims of the Bible but can also critique the extra-Biblical truth claims Amy is making about God.

Amy represents a mind-set that is difficult to surmount. Contemporary culture has largely embraced pluralism, and people who have been immersed in pluralism are prone to take offense at the exclusive claims of Jesus Christ. Were it not so sad, it would be amusing to see how intolerant those who preach tolerance usually are. Some critics might say the portrait of Amy is an inaccurate caricature of pluralism, but I have met enough people like Amy to know that she is not atypical.

The type of religious pluralism espoused by Amy is drastically opposed to the exclusive absolutes of Christianity. In a real way it is just a rehashing of relativism. Relativism is an enticing worldview because it is so easy on the human conscience. Once you accept relativism, you can justify almost anything. This certainly provides an easy escape from the demands of a holy God.

Of course, the problem with relativism is that it is ultimately unworkable. It is the classic "emperor without clothes" worldview. For it to claim that all things (including religion) are relative is to make an absolute claim. The self-refutation is glaring. Joy did her best to ask questions that would bring Amy's contradictions into the light.

Amy's response was to plead a special exception, namely that she be permitted to be intolerant because of the virtue of her particular intolerance. As already noted, it can be difficult to get past this inconsistency when trying to share the gospel with a pluralist.

Religious pluralism is not new, but it became evident in an especially poignant way shortly after the attack on the World Trade Center on September 11, 2001. I remember at least two of the interfaith services receiving national television coverage. Please understand, I completely support and agree with the mind-set of respecting people of other religions, and I do think there is a useful purpose in public displays of tolerance. One of my heroes is Roger Williams, the champion of religious liberty and freedom of conscience in colonial America. When Jesus commanded us to love our neighbors as ourselves, He made it clear just how wide the circle of our neighbors truly is (Luke 10:25–37). My concern is that people like Amy aren't simply advocating respect and freedom. They are actually denying the uniqueness of the Christian gospel and the authority of Jesus' words. This is the error to which Joy was responding.

Joy's questions were designed to expose two things: First, Joy sought to explore Amy's brand of intolerance. Joy was not criticizing Amy for being intolerant (although in Amy's case it was hypocritical). Every person with a conscience believes that certain things must be seen as intolerable. The issue is, What particular things should not be tolerated, and how does anyone know?

The question, How does anyone know? is the second issue Joy sought to explore. Amy was making strong truth claims about God, apparently on her own authority. This attitude is the seedbed of tyranny, the very thing Amy thinks she opposes. Joy brought the conversation to a point where she could share the reason for the hope she has within her (1 Pet. 3:15).

Pluralism is often perilously close to tyranny. The politically correct speech codes on the campus of the typical American university are already attempting to muzzle many Christian campus groups. This condition can now be seen in other settings across America. Learning how to navigate through it is an important task for today's Christian apologists such as Joy.

Thinking It Through

1. Does God hear the prayers of a non-Christian? In what sense does He hear, if at all? What Scripture portions are relevant to this question? Do John 16:23 and 24 preclude the prayers of a non-Christian?

2. If someone in an unreached people group never hears the name of Jesus, can he still go to Heaven under certain conditions? Why or why not? If he can go, what are the necessary conditions?

3. In what ways did Jesus show more tolerance than most of the people around Him? How does John 4:1–42 reflect this tolerance? In what ways did Jesus show less tolerance than

most of the people around Him? How does Matthew 23:1–33 reflect this fact?

Notes

1. The use of the masculine pronoun for God might be objectionable to someone like Amy, but Joy was correct for using it.

ENCOUNTER 9

THE GAY RIGHTS ADVOCATE

UNBELIEVER: Sally, a student at a large state university. Sally advocates a radical feminist ideology that opposes the Biblical worldview.

BELIEVER: Trinity, a fellow student. It is Gay Pride Week on campus, and Trinity will use this opportunity to ask Sally several questions about her worldview.

SALLY: I think the university needs to do even more to promote Gay Pride Week. There are still too many people living in the Dark Ages.

TRINITY: Do you mean that people who do not condone homosexuality need to be encouraged to change their minds?

SALLY: Definitely! There's no room for that kind of intolerance.

TRINITY: Sally, some people oppose homosexuality because they think it is morally wrong. Does that bother you?

SALLY: Yes, it bothers me. I hate that kind of thinking!

TRINITY: Why?

SALLY: What do you mean, why? These right-wing religious homophobes have no right to cram their religion down other people's throats. They're always judging people who disagree with them. I wish they would crawl back under their rocks and keep their fascism to themselves.

TRINITY: Now quit being so evasive and tell me what you really think.

SALLY: Very funny.

TRINITY: Seriously, Sally, you've said some things I'm not sure you actually believe.

SALLY: Of course I believe what I said.

TRINITY: So you think we should not tolerate those who are intolerant of homosexuality?

[Pause]

SALLY: Clever, Trinity. You're trying to say that I'm guilty of the intolerance for which I criticize the homophobes.

TRINITY: Aren't you?

SALLY: This is different. The Religious Right is dangerous. They are a threat to individual freedom. We have the right to suppress their agenda to protect freedom of choice for everyone.

TRINITY: I'm somewhat confused, Sally. You say you oppose intolerance, and for that reason you won't tolerate those you describe as the Religious Right. You say you are a champion of freedom and therefore you want to hinder the Religious Right from using their freedom to express their beliefs. How can this be?

SALLY: I know what you're saying, Trinity, but the problem is you are missing an important distinction. My intolerance, if you want to call it that, is based on the fact that religion ought to be a private matter. As wrong as they are, I grant Christians the right to believe their homophobic ideas. The problem is that rather than exercising their religious beliefs privately, they try to impose them in the public domain.

TRINITY: Do you think the Religious Right, as you call them, ought to adhere to your view that religion is a private matter?

SALLY: Yes, we would all be better off for it.

TRINITY: Does it bother you that you are a hypocrite?

SALLY: What's that supposed to mean?

TRINITY: Sally, you have a view regarding religion. You say religion is a private matter and religious views don't belong in the public arena. But the moment you express this belief, aren't you bringing your religious views into the public domain? You're not keeping them private. Not only are you not keeping them private, aren't you anxious to see others adopt your view? If you want to avoid hypocrisy or a double standard, then you must never say a word about religion. The moment you do, you're violating your own standard. In other words, you want Christians to remain silent about their religious views, but this is the very thing you yourself aren't doing.

SALLY: But I'm limiting my comments to just one idea. The Christians pontificate on all sorts of matters.

TRINITY: So religion is properly discussed publicly if it is limited to just the one item you champion?

SALLY: Yes, we speak publicly just enough to ensure that all else remains private.

TRINITY: So you want others to conform to your views on religion?

SALLY: C'mon, Trinity, I know what you're doing. If I answer your question with a yes, you will portray me as imposing my views of religion on others. If I answer the question with a no, you will portray me as being unfair for criticizing the Christians to begin with.

TRINITY: It's not how I portray you that matters, Sally. How do your own words portray you?

SALLY: Okay, Trinity, I see you actually paid attention when you studied logic in high school, but your clever use of words can't change the fact that I'm right.

TRINITY: Sally, I don't use logic to flippantly win an argument but to clarify the argument and identify the truth. If logic reveals a flaw in my argument, I correct it. I'm not trying to hide behind clever words. I'm seeking to identify what your words mean. If your position is logical, you ought to welcome logical questions about it. If your position is illogical, why should anyone embrace it?

[Several moments of silence]

SALLY: Trinity, you have done a good job defending the Bible-thumpers. Are you a born-again Christian?

TRINITY: Yes, Sally, I am.

SALLY: Hey listen, please don't take my comments personally. You really seem to be pretty cool. If all Christians were like you, things would be a lot better.

TRINITY: All Christians are like me, Sally. We are all sinners saved by God's grace through faith in Jesus Christ. I know the stereotype of Christians you have in mind. With all due respect, Sally, stereotypical thinking is ugly no matter who is doing it.

SALLY: Okay, I'm sorry, Trinity. I know you're different, and I respect you. But I've seen too many Christians who are close-minded bigots. You can't reason with them, and they would rather condemn than love. And I can't stand that.

TRINITY: Sally, it is sad that some people who call themselves Christians do in fact closely conform to your stereotype. Jesus Christ once said that not everyone who claims to be a Christian is the real item, and maybe you've encountered some of those people. All genuine Christians still wrestle with character flaws and sin, and if you get to know me any better, you'll see I'm not perfect either.

SALLY: Trinity, you have far fewer flaws than most of the people I've known. I think you are making a mistake by accepting the shackles of a patriarchal culture.

TRINITY: Sally, you are mistaken. Jesus Christ said that we can find true freedom only when we acknowledge His authority. The issue is not men against women but truth against error. Would you be willing to have me show you what the Bible says about freedom and truth?

SALLY: Well, if I'm going to claim to support tolerance, then I guess I should give you a hearing. Go ahead.

Summary of Trinity and Sally

Sally is typical of people who resent the value system of the Bible. In this brief conversation she seems to fit the label of being politically correct. She rejects what the Bible says about homosexuality, marriage, and other moral issues. She also becomes angry when Christians take a public stand on these moral issues. Trinity responded to this view by showing Sally the inconsistency (hypocrisy) in attacking Christians for making their positions public. Some politically correct people know they are using a double standard and don't care, but others might be open to reevaluating their position if its inherent contradiction is pointed out to them.

Sally also promotes a feminist ideology borne out of a response to male chauvinism and oppression, as well as rebelliousness on the part of feminists. Sally incorrectly attributes male chauvinism to the Bible. The Bible does ordain distinct roles for the sexes, and women are to be submissive in areas established by God. But the Bible gives women a special place of honor that was radical in Bible times (and ours). Husbands are to love their wives as Christ loved the church and gave Himself for her. Men are to submit to the needs of their wives (Eph. 5:21). Think about that! How many men truly place the needs and interests of their wives ahead of their own? Far too many men ignore the Biblical injunctions to recognize the precious value of women and instead seek only their own gratification. Sin affects women too. (How's that for equality?) Militant feminism is as much an act of rebellion against God as is male selfishness. As long as Sally is committed to intellectual autonomy, she will continue to be in darkness. Trinity has tried to show Sally that her position is indefensible.

This encounter is an important one. Many people today have the opinion that it is improper for Christians to take a public stand on moral issues. Rather than be intimidated by this opinion, Christians need to follow Trinity's example and point out the contradiction that exists when people publicly denounce Christians for speaking to the public. This contradiction reinforces our conviction that those who are unwilling to acknowledge the authority of God can never adequately answer the questions created by their commitment to autonomy.

The more Sally spoke, the more evident it became that she is an absolutist and a dogmatist. This is not a criticism. The problem is that she wouldn't acknowledge that the very dogmatism she denounces in Christianity is present in her own worldview. The belief in absolutes for which Christians are criticized is embedded in her own worldview. They are thinly disguised, and Trinity did a good job pointing them out to Sally.

Don't read too much into Sally's use of the term "Religious Right." It is a simple way for the opponents of Christianity to describe politically active conservative evangelicals. Like all labels, it is prone to be inaccurate. Christians also need to be careful about looking for political solutions to spiritual problems. One of the drawbacks of political activism within the evangelical movement is that we inadvertently become known more for the cultural and political things we oppose than for the glorious gospel we believe. Being engaged in the political process can be appropriate, but when Christians are known primarily for their political activism, we have unwittingly subverted the mission Jesus gave to His church.

Finally, take note of how Trinity was able to steer the conversation toward the Bible and the gospel. Sally's deepest need is to know Jesus Christ. Trinity saw the need and had compassion for Sally, even though Trinity could not accept Sally's lifestyle. When Christians debate or argue ("argue" is not a dirty word) with non-Christians, it must be the overflow of hearts filled with compassion and a love for the truth. Many homosexuals have been made the object of hurtful humor, angry denouncements, and personal animosity. Christians must speak truthfully, but there is also a spirit of grace that must season our speech.

Thinking It Through

1. Should Christians use political means to oppose the changes being advocated by the gay rights movement? Why or why not? What Scriptures are germane to this difficult question? How does your position fit into the task of evangelism and apologetics?

2. Is homosexuality a sin from which people need to repent? What Scripture portions teach this truth?

3. Trinity was able to bring the conversation around to Jesus Christ and His teachings on freedom and truth. How could Trinity use this theme to present the gospel to Sally?

4. In John 8:31–41 Jesus used the concepts of freedom and slavery in the realm of sin. How could Trinity correctly apply this passage (especially verse 32) to her presentation of the gospel to Sally?

5. Can you find some examples from Scripture of Jesus showing love and compassion for people whose sin the Bible clearly condemns?

ENCOUNTER 10

THE EASTERN MYSTIC

UNBELIEVER: Vijay, a practitioner of Eastern mysticism. Vijay's beliefs reflect the influence of Hinduism in that he believes reality differs greatly from the traditional Western perception of it.

BELIEVER: Tom, a youth pastor on an outing at a local park with a few of his teens. Tom has learned that Vijay and some of his companions are using the park as a meeting place. After some polite introductions, Vijay and Tom enter the following discussion.

❖ ❖ ❖

TOM: Hello. My name is Tom. And you are?

VIJAY: Vijay.

TOM: It's nice to meet you, Vijay. It's a beautiful day to be in the park, isn't it?

VIJAY: Yes, it is.

TOM: Vijay, was that yoga you were doing?

VIJAY: Yes. Do you understand yoga?

TOM: I don't know too much about it, Vijay, but isn't it something you do as a part of improving your karma as you seek enlightenment?

VIJAY: Well, that's crudely stated, but you are basically correct. You see, we are all part of the One, but we don't all know it. In order to experience Nirvana we need to learn that this world with its distinctions and contrasts is really what we call maya, illusion.

TOM: Vijay, with all due respect I think it is an illusion to believe that all we experience is an illusion. The God Who created you is Himself distinct from the created world. He is a Person, and you need to know Him. The way to Him is through His Son, Jesus Christ, Who said, "I am the way, the truth, and the life. No one comes to the Father except through Me." He died on the cross as payment for sins, and that payment is totally sufficient for those who call on His name.

VIJAY: So you're a Christian. I think Jesus had some good things to say about Oneness. I fear that the religion that bears His name cannot bring true enlightenment. Christians are caught up in maya. Nirvana can come only to those who get past the illusion of that which is not the One.

TOM: Why does escaping maya matter?

VIJAY: Because enlightenment awaits those who understand they are a part of the One.

TOM: Don't worry, Vijay, I have already attained Nirvana. My perception of Nirvana is eating a pepperoni pizza and watching a football game. This is my reality. Isn't this what you are seeking?

VIJAY: You don't understand, Tom. You are still bound to this illusory world you call reality. You need to see that all is One.

TOM: So I'm mistaken in my claim that Nirvana is what I experience eating pizza and watching football?

VIJAY: Yes.

TOM: But if all is One, then isn't my impression that pizza and football is Nirvana also a part of the One?

VIJAY: No, you can't trust your thoughts because you make distinctions in your thinking. These types of distinctions are a part of the bad karma that must be changed so that you can truly be enlightened.

TOM: But, Vijay, how can you categorize my definition of Nirvana as being wrong? To do so, don't you have to focus on particulars and on differences? For you to think of me as being wrong, you have to deny the very thing you say you believe. When I reject what you say, am I not simply participating in the One? Vijay, doesn't your view strike you as being illogical?

VIJAY: Ah, that is your problem, not mine. Logic does not enlighten; it only creates distinctions where none should be.

TOM: Like the distinction between your concept of Nirvana and mine? Your belief that I am wrong is a part of maya—illusion. I know this because you are using logic to distinguish between the two of us.

Ienoughofthisresleeping.I'mdone.

Isn't that the very thing you said ought not to be done?

VIJAY: I refuse to play your games of logic, Tom. It is bad karma and contributes nothing.

TOM: Then are you willing to give up your belief in your religion? You've just said that logic has no place in your religion. Of course, you are using logic to make this distinction. You criticize my commitment to logic. Now if your criticism is logical, you can't use it. If it is illogical, then you're saying that you are committed to being totally irrational. If I say that Nirvana is pizza, football, and the denial of the One, or that Nirvana is raping women and Nirvana is torturing animals, how can you disagree with me without simultaneously exhibiting a belief in logic, distinctions, and differences?

VIJAY: You are so caught up in bad karma that there is no value in talking to you.

TOM: I'm not trying to be disrespectful, Vijay. Nor am I trying to confuse you. But the moment you label me as having bad karma, you yourself are denying Oneness. You are convinced that I am still in maya, but you think this because you are making distinctions and drawing comparisons. But distinctions and comparisons require logic, yet you said logic has no place in your religion because it is a part of maya. It seems that for you to disagree with me means that you believe in truth and error and right and wrong. But if these categories of thought belong in the world of maya, why don't you give up your objections and experience the Oneness that we share? Why not simply accept the fact that Nirvana is what I say it is?

VIJAY: Like I said, there is no value in talking to you. Nirvana is nothing like what you are saying.

TOM: But, Vijay, am I not simply using the tools you gave me? If logic and distinctions are not valid, why should I think that raping women is not a legitimate function of the eternal One?

VIJAY Do you really believe it is okay to rape women?

TOM: No I don't, Vijay. But my opposition to rape is consistent with my beliefs; your opposition to rape is not consistent with your beliefs.

VIJAY: Why not?

TOM: Because if becoming enlightened means that all distinctions disappear within the One, then you also lose the distinction between good and evil.

VIJAY: As people become enlightened, they will stop doing the acts that relate to maya, including rape.

TOM: If I say rape is the path to enlightenment, how can you dispute it without making distinctions?

VIJAY: I don't think we are getting anywhere, Tom. We should agree to disagree.

TOM: My prayer for you, Vijay, is that you will give thought to what we discussed today. Jesus Christ alone can set you free from the true slave master, sin. Sin is not maya, Vijay. It is all too real. The way to be at peace with the world around us is to be at peace with the God Who made us. The way has been opened through the death of Jesus on the cross for our sins, and through His resurrection.

VIJAY: I can't accept that.

TOM: Vijay, I pray that you will someday. But since we do disagree, I want to thank you for still talking with me. I hope we can talk again someday soon.

Summary of Tom and Vijay

Eastern mysticism is a big umbrella under which I include Hinduism, Buddhism, New Age thinking, and several other similar religions. Christians need to understand that there are numerous variations within these large world religions. It is not the purpose of this volume to interact with them in-depth. Several well-researched treatments of Eastern religions have been written from a Christian apologetical perspective. Readers interested in further study are encouraged to seek those sources.[1]

This encounter has been included to demonstrate that rational apologetics is possible with people such as Vijay. As complex and varied as Eastern mysticism is, a few key concepts are present in many Eastern systems. The first one is monism. Monism is a technical term for the view of reality that sees all things as being one. It views distinctions and particulars as illusions and claims that enlightenment comes when a person gets beyond the illusion of individualism and becomes absorbed in the One. Reincarnation is often seen as the mechanism by which the individual progresses through various phases until reaching Nirvana, the sense of losing one's identity as a particular and instead becoming, as it were, a drop of water falling into the "shoreless" ocean.

Pain and suffering are a part of maya, the illusion that most Westerners think of as being the real world, or reality. According to Eastern mysticism, the greatest sufferers are in the state of suffering because of bad karma. This belief is one of the primary reasons Hinduism has shown such little concern for the suffering of people stuck in the lower castes of society in India. The

Western mind-set is to fix these kinds of social ills because they are perceived as being real concerns in a real world. In a sense one could say the typical Westerner wants to improve the present reality; the typical Easterner wants to transcend reality.

Please understand that this summary is general and should not be seen as applying across the board. It is merely a good starting point for understanding Eastern mysticism.

A second major theme in Eastern mysticism is a rejection of logic. Ideally logic should not be called a Western domain because logic is not simply a cultural distinction. Logic is central to how God has created the world, and we should avoid giving the impression that it is merely a preference for one culture and is not a preference for another culture. The fact remains, however, that logic is unimportant if not actually disdained in Eastern mysticism. If this disdain strikes you as sounding similar to postmodernism, a common ground does exist. We can trace the rise of Eastern mysticism in America to approximately the same time that postmodernism began to have a significant presence: the 1960s.

Logic is frowned upon because it depends so heavily on distinctions, particulars, and contrasts. If you believe that these categories of thought are maya (illusion), then logic should be rejected.

A third distinction of Eastern thought is pantheism, the view that all is God. The trees, the grass, the animals the sky, the water—all of these things together are God. Actually it is better to call it "god," since pantheism does not think of a personal God as Christianity does. Remember that there are hundreds of millions of practitioners of various forms of Eastern mysticism, and it is a mistake to think they are all pantheistic.

These three distinctions—monism, a rejection of logic, and pantheism—characterize some of what you might encounter when dealing with a practitioner of certain Eastern religions.

What about the encounter between Tom and Vijay? Tom had a basic understanding of Vijay's beliefs. Tom also recognized two things about Vijay that Vijay does not know about himself: Vijay has been created in the image of God, and Vijay lives in the objectively real world that God created. Calling these things maya, or illusion, does not mean they do not exist. Tom understands that Vijay cannot escape the way God has made him and the world in which he lives.

For Vijay to reject Tom's beliefs, he had to use tools that are consistent with Christianity but are inconsistent with mysticism. Human language is not even possible without logic; this is another function of the way God has made us. Vijay also could not escape the need for making distinctions and comparisons. Yet if Vijay's worldview were true, he could not draw distinctions between different experiences within the One. The bottom line is that Vijay's worldview cannot provide the preconditions necessary for truth, logic, science, morality, medicine, and language. Every time Vijay uses one of these things, he is borrowing from Christianity.

It is possible for Vijay to completely reject Tom's appeal because fundamentally the conflict is one of spiritual darkness and the condition of the human heart. Tom made sure that Vijay heard the truth claims of Jesus Christ. Vijay immediately rejected the gospel because of his worldview commitments. When that happened, Tom sought to "answer a fool according to his folly" (Prov. 26:5) by demonstrating the internal inconsistency and impossibility of Vijay's worldview. Vijay's attempt to denigrate logic is a telling indictment against Eastern mysticism, whether Vijay acknowledges it or not. (No one who denigrates logic and then seeks to justify his rejection of logic should be allowed to go unchallenged.)

Thinking It Through

1. In what ways did Vijay unconsciously reflect the fact that he bears the image of God?

2. Genesis 1 and 2 clearly portray God as a personal Being distinct from the created world. Where do you find this teaching in the New Testament?

3. In what way does Vijay's understanding of reality resemble the people described in Romans 1:21–24?

4. Near the end of the encounter Tom plainly stated the gospel, even though Vijay hadn't given up his pantheism. What are some passages that speak of the ability of God's Word to overcome such unbelief?

5. As different as they are, Tom and Vijay both have a sense of the eternal. What does Ecclesiastes 3:11 say about this sense?

Notes

1. For the Christian reader who anticipates having extensive contact with practitioners of Hinduism, New Age thought, and other related systems, additional study is recommended. Many people with an Eastern perspective do not share Vijay's beliefs. To be fair with them, it is useful to study more extensively.

A TRUE-LIFE EXAMPLE

THE encounters you have just read are fictional. The encounter you are about to read is a word-for-word account of a real-life conversation that took place in front of more than eight hundred people. On February 25, 2005, I had the privilege of participating in a public debate with an atheist. The debate was held at my church, in conjunction with what we called the Worldview Conference. This forum gave me a unique opportunity to make use of ATW.

Both of us were given two segments to state the case for our particular beliefs. Then we were allotted six minutes each to cross-examine our opponent based on what was said in the first two segments. Printed here is my six-minute cross-examination of the atheist spokesman.

Each of the fictional encounters you have just read was written long before this debate took place. Indeed, most of them were written several years before this debate. I point out this fact because the exchange that took place in the public debate is a remarkable parallel to the content in the fictional encounters.

Many non-Christians attended the debate, but the atmosphere was cordial. My opponent and his friends sensed that they received respect, courtesy, and a warm welcome. I was proud of my church family.

Appendix C (p. 225) is a transcript of the opening presentation in a similar debate I had several years earlier. Both debates reflect the same approach, so reading appendix C will give you a close approximation of the setting for the following encounter. Again, what follows here is the cross-examination portion of the debate from our Worldview Conference.

JAY: Do you think—I would simply like a yes or no at this point—do you believe that Hitler was wrong in his actions?

MICHAEL: Yes.

JAY: Okay, thank you. My second question then would be, Why was he wrong?

MICHAEL: Well again, there are objective frameworks of morality that one can create. For example it is possible for morality to come about via evolutionary processes. We can see various moral behavior, for example, in populations of chimpanzees, and the reason it is possible for this to occur, of course, is because morality creates cooperative societies, and it is more efficient to live in a cooperative society than it is to live in a society full of conflict.

JAY: [*I cut in at this point because of time constraints.*]

Michael, what if an individual has no desire to be cooperative? Is he not free to choose lack of co-operation?

MICHAEL: Certainly an individual could choose not to be co-operative. However, we are social animals; chimpanzees are social animals. When an individual is not cooperative, when an individual does not cooperate with the group, there are often ramifications for that. And in a cooperative society, which is more efficient than a conflicting society, it increases survival benefits if the individuals can work together.

JAY: If I was a member of the German resistance in 1944 and was opposed to the larger social cooperative of Nazi Germany. I would be, as an individual, going against the majority. Why would I be wrong?

MICHAEL: Well I disagree that you would be an individual going against the majority because, in fact, if you look at the world's reaction to Nazi Germany, the majority was most definitely against Hitler, and there was a world war over that.

JAY: Are you saying, then, that the test for morality is the majority?

MICHAEL: Well, that's part of the test. I mean, there are different sorts of social groups, and there are different kinds of violations of morality that take place. For example, in the Bible in the Ten Commandments you have rules against—do not do this thing, do not do that thing to your neighbor. Now this is a great example of in-group morality which was common at the time, and, in fact, if you did something to an outsider in that culture, there was a different standard. So yes, there are different standards of morality depending on the scope of the social group you are referring to.

JAY: Let's say that over the next twenty years the nature of human opinion changes such that 95 percent of all living people believe that the best thing that could happen would be the extermination of the Jews. Would those 95 percent be wrong and, if so, on what basis?

MICHAEL: Well, let's see. Would they be wrong based upon, for example, the extermination of the Amalekites? Certainly you can't look to the Bible to find that it's wrong to exterminate a particular population, because the example is right there ordered by God. Now what you can do, however, is look at things like empathy, and you could look at things like the increase of human suffering, which must have been very large considering the drowning of the whole world. There was certainly a lot of suffering going on there.

JAY: Michael, you have clearly rejected the moral basis provided in the Bible, and at this point that's not what's being debated. I'm trying to explore your basis for morality. If morality can somehow be the result of evolution, then why can't we say that Hitler's morality was the result of how evolution affected him? Why would his evolutionary moral code be wrong and somebody else's moral code, also the result of evolution, be right?

MICHAEL: Again there's a different standard. I mean history shows us that the overall view of Hitler was wrong.

Now there are other standards. We can certainly learn from Hitler. We can learn about things such as excess nationalism. Here again we go back to an objective standard and learn from our mistakes, something we seem to have done through slavery, even though the Bible condones it. And so again, we do have an objective ability to look at the effects of different policies and thoughts on different human beings, and we can learn from those mistakes and live in a world and create a world that is—

JAY: *[I cut in at this point because of time constraints.]* In our last few seconds, your understanding of the meaning of the word "objective" as it is applied to morality is completely irrational. How can morality be objective if it is created by man?

MICHAEL: Well, it's objective in the sense that we have observations that are looked at and examined and then looked at again by others and compared. You know, the purpose of objectivity in science, for example, is to eliminate the error that comes from subjectivity, and that generally comes from cross-examination of other observations.

JAY: You are equivocating on the meaning of the word objective—that is not what the word means.

[Time expired at this point.]

Summary

Those six minutes passed too quickly! I wish time had permitted us to explore the accuracy and the implications of Michael's answers. With all due respect to Michael, his answers were weak, and they left him wide open to refutation. Don't misunderstand. Michael is an intelligent man. I suppose that if he had had more time, he might have worded his answers differently; but I don't think he had any way of escaping the inherent weakness of atheism. If time had permitted, I would have tried to dig a little deeper.

The first question I asked was a standard test case. Of course Hitler was wrong. Michael and I agreed on that. But the questions were designed to explore the foundation upon which Michael was standing when he condemned Hitler. That is why I asked the second question, why was he wrong?

It is here that Michael's worldview lacks consistency. First of all, one does not "create objective frameworks of morality."[1] If we create it ourselves, then it is subjective, and this subjectivity leaves us vulnerable to all the inconsistencies of moral relativism. The atheist worldview has a difficult time justifying any objective basis for morality.

Second, Michael turned to evolution as a possible basis for morality. See the summary of the sixth encounter, "The Secular Humanist" (p. 141), and the entire text of the third encounter, "The Evolutionist" (p. 97). Of course, the keystone proposition of evolution is *change*. If evolution eventually takes us in the direction of Hitler, would Nazism then be acceptable? If you choose evolution as a foundation, how can you, with any consistency, use categories of good and evil, right and wrong? Such categorizations ring hollow if morality is the result of evolution (time and chance acting on matter).

From there, Michael then asserted that "morality creates cooperative societies, and it is more efficient to live in a cooperative society than it is to live in a society full of conflict." This proposition is filled with logical fallacies and arbitrary assertions. To say that "morality creates" is to use the term "morality" in a way that is almost nonsensical. Just moments before Michael had said "we create objective frameworks of morality." Then he said morality creates society. I think he might word this differently if given an opportunity to restate it, but this rewording would not correct the glaring flaw in his proposition.

He used value-laden words such as "cooperative" and "efficient." These words are acceptable if one is describing various parts that go together to make an internal combustion engine work. Things don't fit nearly as neatly when describing human beings. I find no delight in making the following assertion, and I am sure Michael would not like it, but it fits within his proposition: A society is more efficient (and cooperation would be enhanced) if we euthanize all people over the age of seventy, all those with mental or physical disabilities, and, finally, all those who have severe illnesses that are a drain on our medical resources. In addition, any individual unable to meet our chosen standard of intelligence will be sterilized so as not to give birth to undesirable children who would hinder our efficiency and our cooperation as a society.

Based on his presuppositions, Michael would have no consistent basis for rejecting my model. The fact that he would personally dislike it is irrelevant.

Michael's answers got progressively worse. His next proposition was that the "survival benefits" to a society provide standards of morality. By now I would hope that the reader sees the folly in this standard. The lifeboat scenario in the seventh encounter, "The Values Clarifier" (p. 159), exposes the disastrous consequences of Michael's position. Who gets to define "survival benefits"? Hitler certainly believed he was enhancing the survival benefits of Germany. If he had won the war and exterminated all of his enemies, his actions would have been vindicated according to Michael's view! I know Michael would object to this conclusion, but his appeal to survival benefits leaves this unpleasant door wide open.

As I continued to ask Michael questions, he resorted to an evasion tactic of attacking the Bible's moral code. Such attacks depend upon misrepresentations (or, to be charitable, misunderstandings) of the Biblical record, but they were out of place in a cross-examination that was designated to explore the rational basis for his position. He was free to ask me for a theodicy during his cross-examination of me, and if he had, I would have gladly given it.

Although much more could be written in a critique of Michael's answers (his appeal to chimpanzee society is an inviting target), a final observation will be made in response to his assertion that we have an objective standard by which we can "learn from our mistakes." But, of course, that's the very thing the atheist worldview cannot provide. Was Hitler's mistake that he had the wrong values or that his foolish military strategy kept him from finishing what he started?

The Christian worldview provides what the atheist worldview cannot: an objective standard for judging mistakes. The unbeliever might not accept the Christian worldview as being true, but at least it can provide a justification for believing that objective standards exist. How can we encourage unbelievers to consider the Christian worldview? Ask them why.

Notes

1. The term "objective" has several meanings in language and philosophy. We sometimes ask someone else for an objective opinion. By this we mean that we want to avoid opinions flavored by our own internal emotions or by individual experience. We can use "objective" as pointing to an external nonhuman reality such as, "The temperature in this room is 38 degrees Fahrenheit." This is objective. But if I were to say, "I am chilly," I would be introducing an individualized human element that is subjective in nature.

This is why I questioned Michael's statement that "there are objective frameworks of morality that one can create." Two people can agree that the temperature is 38 degrees. There is an objective nature to this proposition. But one person can be chilly while the other is quite comfortable. We would not say that one of them must be wrong, for they are stating their own personal experiences, which are subjective in nature. One man is correct when he says he is chilly; the other man is correct when he says he is comfortable.

Now, if morality is something we create, how can it be anything other than subjective? I agree that objective morality can exist—but only because we don't create it; its source is external to us. The Christian worldview can account for the existence of objective morality; the atheist worldview cannot. And if morality is the result of evolution, one cannot argue for "oughtness." (I ought to be kind to my neighbor; I ought not sleep with his wife.)

Michael repeatedly appealed to the objective nature of morality, even though his espoused worldview undermines any basis for morality that is external or objective. In so doing, he was exhibiting his God-given conscience as explained in Romans 2:14 and 15.

APPENDIX A

THE CHRISTIAN WORLDVIEW

THE term "worldview" has, in recent years, become a familiar one to many people. However, hearing a term used does not necessarily indicate that a person understands its meaning. This appendix, intended to provide a simple working knowledge of worldviews, considers (1) a general description of a worldview, (2) the Christian worldview, and (3) testing worldviews.

General Description

Every thinking person has a worldview, whether he is aware of it or not. A worldview is the core set of beliefs by which a person interprets all that he experiences in life. These beliefs operate at a foundational level in our thinking. In fact, they are so basic that we often rely upon them without consciously thinking about what we are doing, much as we continually breathe without even being fully aware of it.

Central Elements of a Worldview

What are the central elements of a person's worldview? In general terms, we will identify five major areas that make up a worldview. They are beliefs about five topics:

God—Is there a God? Can He/She/It be known? What is He like?

Reality—What is real? Is the universe eternal? Is everything interrelated and connected or separate and distinct? Does beauty exist?

Knowledge—How do we know what we know? Is what we learn through our senses reliable? What is the relationship between faith and reason?

Ethics—What is good or moral? Can moral judgments be made? By what standard? Why should someone seek to be good?

Humankind—Does mankind make free choices, or are choices determined by factors such as environment, God, or genetics? Are humans material only, or do they also possess an immaterial soul? Is there a purpose to life? Does a person discover it externally or create it internally? Does existence continue after death?

Sample of a Worldview in Daily Life

Although these five areas can involve complex questions and answers that cause endless debates among philosophers, theologians, scientists, and so forth, they are also practical. Let's use Jane as an example. Jane is late for work, so she is speeding. Should she feel guilty? As she approaches a stop sign, she estimates the needed distance to stop. How does she know? She has driven past here every day for a month. Without consciously thinking about it, Jane is confident that the same physical laws that slowed her car at a certain rate yesterday function exactly the same way today.

At the intersection, a car driven by another motorist almost hits Jane. Alarmed by the near-accident and relieved to be safe she exclaims, "Thank God." Is there a God to hear this utterance?

Does this God exert an influence over the behavior of cars (or their drivers) at busy intersections?

Jane is tired. A painful back for the last week has made it nearly impossible to sleep. Fighting to stay alert as she drives, she thinks she sees a deer standing by the side of the road. Yet as she prepares to swerve, the deer seems to have disappeared. Was it really there, or did she imagine it?

This is not how Jane wanted to start her day. Late for work and with an aching back, she is so tired she has had a near-accident, and now she is possibly imagining deer waiting to run across the road. Is any job really worth this aggravation? Does life have a purpose beyond paying the current month's bills?

Jane will interpret these experiences through her worldview. Under her present circumstances she probably isn't consciously examining her worldview commitments. She is simply trying to get to work on time. However, her drive to work has caused her, consciously or not, to interact with the five basic elements previously mentioned: God, reality, knowledge, ethics, and humankind.

Change of Worldview, Change of Perception

It might be helpful to think of worldviews as being similar to wearing prescription sunglasses. How you see and understand the things around you is directly related to the glasses through which you are looking. Change the prescription (the worldview), and you see things differently. Every thinking person is wearing worldview sunglasses, but we see things differently from people who have different worldviews.

It is important to recognize that, unlike sunglasses, worldview beliefs are not easily changed. If today I think pizza is my favorite food, but tomorrow I think seafood is better, I haven't really tinkered with the foundational beliefs of my worldview. But if today I profess to be an atheist, and tomorrow I change my mind and believe God created the heavens and the earth, I have drastically altered my worldview at the core level. How I interpret life experiences next week will be much different because my worldview has substantially changed. Considered in this way, it makes sense to conclude that a spiritual conversion involves a fundamental shift in worldview thinking.

Remember, everyone has a worldview. This doesn't mean that everyone has given careful thought to his worldview or can even articulate exactly what it is he believes (and why he believes it). Humanly speaking, one of the great needs in effective communication with others (including evangelistic communication) is learning how to identify someone else's worldview beliefs.

The Christian Worldview
The Biblical Command for a Christian Worldview

It goes without saying that Christians disagree with one another over many points of theology and interpretation of the Bible. Although all theology is important, many disputes are far enough away from core, or basic, beliefs so that the disputed beliefs can be changed, corrected, or refined without seriously affecting the Christian worldview. A thorough reading of the Bible indicates that God has commanded Christians to learn to think in accordance with the Christian worldview. The command to think accordingly requires that we give careful thought to our core assumptions and bring them into alignment with God's Word.

I believe we can illustrate this command through a paraphrase of Romans 12:1 and 2: "Christians, since God has been so merciful to us, we should give all that we are and all that we have to Him. Our self-sacrifice to Him should be pure so that we please Him. Doing this makes sense. It's time that we reject the worldviews that the unbelieving world influences us to accept. Instead, let's allow God to so change how we think, that our worldview perfectly conforms with God's Word. Then we will know how best to please Him." How we think matters!

The Christian Worldview in Daily Life

We Christians often fail to think in terms of the Christian worldview in many areas of life. Yes, there is a distinctly Christian way to think about finances, cancer, art, human rights, law, entertainment, politics, exercise, education, psychology, sex, history, the environment, sports, relationships, tsunamis, religions, the weather, children, medicine, philosophy, ethics, authority, literature, music, marriage, science, employees, employers, and on and on and on!

We must avoid the ever-present danger of compartmental thinking. By this I refer to our tendency to place our Christian faith within one compartment of our lives, isolated and distinct from other compartments. A classic (and controversial) example of this mind-set is the politician who professes to be pro-life but won't endorse legislation banning partial birth abortion. He explains this irony as being appropriate because his religious convictions are a private matter. Thus his political life and his Christianity are kept in separate compartments. Another example is the college student who, though being a Christian, joins her classmates in cheating on an exam because it is standard operating procedure. How about the Christian basketball coach who incessantly badgers the referee because badgering the ref is, after all, just a part of the game? The Christian worldview teaches us to see things differently. We see the world and interpret all that we experience through the filter provided by our core beliefs in the five key areas.

Core Beliefs

What are the core beliefs of the Christian worldview? Biblically and historically understood, they are as follows:

God—God is the eternally self-existent creator of the universe. Although He actively sustains the universe, He is separate and distinct from it. He controls all that comes to pass according to His unchanging attributes.

Reality—Reality is what corresponds to what God has freely created. That which is real can be experienced through the bodies and the minds God has given to us, aided by God's willingness to reveal these things to us.

Knowledge—Knowledge is possible because of how God has made both us and the universe in which we live. There are several ways we come to know things (our senses, experiences, reason, conscience), but all true knowledge is ultimately dependent upon God (Prov. 1:7), whether the creature acknowledges Him or not (Rom. 1:18-21).

Ethics—Ethics, or that which is good, reflects the character of God. God is the standard of good by which all things are measured, and His standards are directly revealed through His Word and are also partially known through human conscience (Rom. 2:14, 15). The human capacity to think and act as a moral being is complicated by the presence of sin.

Humankind—Humankind (each individual human) bears the image of God, and thus has great significance and great potential. The human condition has been greatly damaged by the sin nature that we all have, yet each individual remains accountable to God for the choices he makes. Man has both physical and nonphysical (the soul) aspects, and finds his ultimate purpose in knowing, enjoying, and glorifying God. To be in proper relation with God, men and women must acknowledge their sin and believe on the Lord Jesus Christ according to the Biblical presentation of the gospel message.

Testing Worldviews

The Christian worldview teaches us to examine, test, challenge, and judge other worldviews (1 Thess. 5:21). Of course, this practice is currently politically incorrect because of the pervasive influence of postmodernism on many people's worldviews. Within Christian circles there is a complex debate over how best to critique worldviews and how best to defend and justify the Christian worldview.

Three Tests

In the most simple of ways, I would suggest that three basic tests are especially helpful:

Conformity to the Bible—Yes, this claim is obvious, but it is also rationally defensible.

Logical coherence—For example, some worldviews espouse extreme moral relativism. "There are no absolutes!" is the cry. My question would be, Oh really? Are you absolutely sure? The lack of internal coherence is a telling criticism. I once took a graduate seminar in history at the secular university I was attending. Commenting upon her view of history, one of the other graduate students said, "I don't believe in facts." If I had been quicker, I would have asked her, "Is that a fact?" Of course, she was using the term somewhat differently, but ultimately, when subjected to an internal critique, her worldview lacked logical coherence.

Workability—Pragmatism cannot stand alone as a test for truth, but it can be helpful. Does the worldview in question provide meaningful answers for humankind's ultimate concerns? (Here are just three questions: Does life have meaning? Why is there evil? Why is there something rather than nothing?) Taken as a whole, the Christian worldview surpasses all other worldviews.

Summary

Christians are commanded to love God with all their heart, soul, *mind*, and strength (Mark 12:30). We can fulfill this command with much greater effectiveness as we grow in our understanding of the Christian worldview.

APPENDIX B

PRESUPPOSITIONALISM

S AN explanation of presuppositionalism, this appendix is somewhat limited. Within the presuppositionalist camp there are variations; therefore, I would not be surprised to hear some presuppositionalists say that the ATW method as described in this book is not true presuppositionalism. I am not protective of the label. Labels make useful servants, but they are terrible masters. If ATW is not fully consistent with how others define presuppositionalism, I won't lose any sleep over it.

Presuppositionalism Defined

Presuppositionalism is exactly what its name suggests: Christian truth is to be presupposed from the outset, not arrived at through the independent use of human reason. If the existence of God and the revelation of God contained in the Bible are not presupposed, then men will always be learning but never finding (2 Tim. 3:7; Prov. 1:7; 28:26; Eph. 4:17, 18).

Reasons to Presuppose the Faith

There are two major reasons for defending the faith by pre-supposing it. First, the Bible condemns an approach to knowledge that calls for neutrality. The universe belongs to God, and in Christ is all true knowledge (Col. 2:3). The spirit of our age suggests that in the name of fairness and open-mindedness, Christians should set aside their faith commitments and look at the evidence for or against God in a spirit of neutrality. We are supposed to let the evidence speak for itself and not impose our prior faith commitments or presuppositions upon it. But this action is contrary to Scripture. It is also the trap Eve fell into (Gen. 3:1–6). As Christians we believe in the sovereign authority of the Godhead and the moral obligation of every knee to bow (Phil. 2:9–11). We are being inconsistent if our arguments, which are intended to prove the lordship of Jesus Christ, employ a method that denies Him His rightful place at the outset (see 1 Peter 3:15).

We can't reason backwards in an endless stream of arguments. At some point we reach an ultimate authority or presupposition by which we argue for other things. This ultimate authority is the God of the Bible. If we attempt to prove Him by using something else, then that something else is actually more ultimate or primary than God. This approach cannot truly glorify God, and it has the added flaw of being inherently contradictory (arguing for the ultimacy of God by using something other than God). Whatever that something is takes precedence over the God we claim to believe is ultimate. In 1 Peter 3:15 Peter described the apologist's task as beginning with setting apart Christ as Lord of our hearts (thoughts). Proverbs 1:7 states that the fear of the Lord is the beginning of knowledge.

The second major reason for defending the faith by presupposing it is that if we do not build our case by the use of presuppositions, we are surrendering our strongest weapon. If we assume there is no God and then honestly consider where that leaves us, (we would see that knowledge, science, ethics, and logic would be impossible. Atheism and other worldviews make use of these things, but they cannot account for them.) In a real sense unbelievers are presupposing the Christian worldview inwardly, even while they argue against it externally. Romans 1:18–20 addresses this act of self-deception and suppression.

Human Reason

The ATW method is an attempt to take the essence of presuppositionalism and demonstrate one possible application of it in evangelism. The ATW method does not deny the use of human reason. Rather, it is an attempt to show that human reason that does not acknowledge and submit to God and His Word can never justify itself. Human reason is a gift from God and a reflection of our being created in God's image (Gen. 1:26). However, human reason is reliable only when it bows on bended knee before the Creator. If God is not presupposed from the outset, human reason will always end in confusion. Our inability to devise a truly satisfactory system of ethics apart from God is one example of the inevitability of confusion.

We can reason with unbelievers (Acts 17:2) because they, too, were created in the image of God. But we must always remember that they are sinners who cannot be changed by "reason" unless the Holy Spirit intervenes (Acts 13:48). We make use of their reason to expose it as untenable if it is divorced from God (Prov. 26:5).

Sinful Autonomy

We should be cautious when appealing to unbelievers with historical evidences. I believe the evidence for Christianity is impressive, and we can make use of it. But something about unbelievers acting as judge and jury should give us pause.

If we grant unbelievers their autonomy for any other reason

than to show that their reasoning is foolishness, we have diminished the lordship of Christ as the fountain of knowledge (Prov. 1:7). The autonomy of unbelievers is not neutral; it is rooted in rebellion against God (Col. 2:8).

For this reason we must not underestimate the necessity of confronting unbelievers at the source of their unbelief—their presuppositions. As already noted in this appendix, many people, including some Christians, advocate that we let the evidence speak for itself and not impose our prior faith commitments upon it. Not only does this call for suspending our submission to the lordship of Jesus Christ (a sinful attitude), but it simply denies what we know about human nature. We interpret evidence with preexisting attitudes, assumptions, experiences, and expectations.

Presuppositions Color Perception and Interpretation

Consider the spectacle of the O. J. Simpson murder trial. There seemed to be solid evidence to suggest that Simpson had indeed murdered Nicole Brown Simpson and Ron Goldman. Overall, a majority of Americans were persuaded by this evidence, yet a significant number of African Americans were not (if the polling data can be trusted). Both groups saw the same evidence, but it is as though they were wearing two different sets of "worldview sunglasses" and thus arrived at two different conclusions.[1]

Let me admit to one of my presuppositions. Because of my interpretation of Scripture, I do not believe UFOs are extraterrestrial aliens. Although I might be mistaken, I believe the Bible teaches that man has a unique place in the universe and that the only other truly rational creatures are angels. Thus if I were presented with evidence of UFOs, I would interpret it to be either unexplained natural phenomena (odd weather conditions, reflections, and so on), misinterpreted human activity (weather balloons, stealth fighter, and so forth), or demonic activity intended to deceive. Thus the interpretive principles or commitments that

I have negate belief in extraterrestrial aliens, and I am unpersuaded by evidence that others find to be compelling. For me to accept a belief in aliens would require something akin to a religious conversion! The recognition of this dynamic in human belief systems points to the need for presuppositional apologetics.

Historical Evidence

What about the historical evidences upon which some apologists rely? Evidence abounds for the historical reliability of the Gospels and the physical resurrection of Jesus. As a student of history I have frequently been blessed in my study of the evidence that supports the Bible. Presuppositionalism is not opposed to the use of such evidence. Sometimes the Holy Spirit has so prepared the hearts of unbelievers that these evidences are the catalyst for genuine conversions. Sharing these evidences with unbelievers can serve as a litmus test to see if they are committed to autonomy. The rejection of Christian evidence will verify that unbelievers are thinking autonomously and thus need to have their close presuppositions challenged.

A particularly startling example of the limitations of evidence can be found in statements made by atheist scholar Kai Neilsen. He made his comments during a formal debate with Christian apologist J. P. Moreland at the University of Mississippi in 1988. Neilsen claimed that God cannot be detected and that atheism is, therefore, justified. In the following excerpt, notice how easily he dismissed evidence for the resurrection of Jesus:

> Jesus, let us suppose—I don't know much about such things and to be perfectly frank, I'm not terribly interested in them, but let us just suppose it were the case that Jesus raised from the dead. Suppose you collected the bones, and they together in some way reconstituted the living Jesus. Suppose something like that really happened. Suppose

there were good historical evidence for it. I have
no idea if there is or isn't; I suspect for anything
like that, there isn't very good evidence, but let
us assume there is. This wouldn't show there was
an infinite intelligible being. It wouldn't give you
any way of being able to detect if there is a God.
It would be just that a very strange happening
happened, namely, that somebody who died—or
certainly appeared to have died—came together
again as a living human being.[2]

Not only did Neilsen state that he was not persuaded by the
evidence for the resurrection of Jesus, but he also revealed that
his worldview is so controlling that by his own admission he is
not even interested in considering the evidence. Why? Because
he already "knows" God doesn't exist. If Jesus did rise from the
dead, it would be a strange event, but it would say nothing about
the supernatural. While this problem should not discourage
Christians from knowing and using historical evidences, it ought
to alert us to the necessity of combating flawed worldviews on
the presuppositional level. Also, do Neilsen's words remind you of
something Jesus once said? Luke 16:19-31 records Jesus' parable
about a rich man who died and went to Hell. The man begged
someone to warn his living brothers to repent. The man's request
was turned down. He was told that they would not be convinced
even if someone were to rise from the dead (v. 31).

Historical evidences can be useful in supporting the faith of
Christians. Evidentialism has encouraged many Christian students
who have had their faith attacked and criticized by antagonistic
teachers. I have passed many pleasant hours being edified by
reading the research of Christian evidentialists.

Whether the evidences are being used to challenge unbelievers or to encourage believers, we must remember that no
creature has the right to sit in judgment over the Lord, as though
He needs to prove Himself worthy of the belief of fallen man.

This is the potential danger of the misuse of evidences. ATW avoids this danger by putting the burden upon the unbeliever to justify his use of logic, moral absolutes, science, and so forth. We never want to needlessly offend people, but if they are offended by the lordship of Christ, so be it.

Presuppositionalism is not limited to combating atheism or agnosticism. It can be used to scrutinize any worldview, including non-Christian religious worldviews.

One last thing that bears mentioning: Christians from several different schools of apologetics have been used of God, and I am honored to have them as my brothers and sisters in Christ. There has yet to be a perfect Christian this side of Heaven, and we are all blessed to know that God is willing to use jars of clay (2 Cor. 4:7). May Christian apologists of every stripe show charity and humility as we seek to sharpen one another and be sharpened for the glory of God (Prov. 27:17).

Notes

1. It is not my intention to explore the specifics of this racially charged situation, and I trust the reader will not get sidetracked. The purpose of the illustration is to point out the difficulty of neutrality. Being aware of someone's presuppositions can help us strive to be as neutral as possible so our biases do not blind us. However, as Christians we recognize that when it comes to the spiritually charged issue of a person's standing before a holy God, people will, at best, pretend neutrality, and the sin nature will always negate neutrality. (See Jeremiah 17:9, 1 Corinthians 1:18, 2 Corinthians 4:4, and Romans 3:10-18.)

2. The transcript of the debate and related material are available in book form. See J. P. Moreland and Kai Neilsen, *Does God Exist?* (Nashville: Thomas Nelson Publishers, 1990).

APPENDIX C

MY DEBATE WITH AN ATHEIST

O NE of my most rewarding experiences took place when I participated in a formal debate on the campus of a public university in the state of Pennsylvania. What you are about to read is the transcript of my opening presentation in the debate. I hope you will see that I debated in a manner consistent with ATW. The debate occurred in March 1997. It was a golden opportunity to declare the gospel and to evaluate the effectiveness of ATW. Because the setting was formal, I could not freely ask questions the way one would in a friendly conversation. However, the basic philosophy of ATW was the foundation of my presentation.

The debate went well. After giving it careful thought, I have decided to change the name of my opponent and withhold the name of the university. I hope the reason for these changes will be clear after I explain how the debate came to be in the first place.

My brother-in-law was teaching history in a Christian school near the university. Jim is open about his faith, and over a period of years he had written many letters to the editor of his local newspaper. They were usually responses to other letters the newspaper had printed from university professors or one particularly belligerent atheist who lived in the same area. From time to time Jim would ask me to contribute a letter in defense of the Christian worldview. I was a pastor living in upstate New York, but the Pennsylvania-based newspaper did print one or two of my letters.

Eventually I grew frustrated with the limitations of using the newspaper's letters-to-the-editor section to rebut the anti-Christian letters that sometimes appeared. So after much prayer, I wrote a letter to the chairperson of the philosophy department and proposed a formal yet friendly debate with one of the faculty. The initial response was positive, and I looked forward to developing the plans for staging a debate on campus.

Then came an unforeseen development. The faculty of the philosophy department decided to have their brightest student debate from the atheist point of view. This student, whom I will call Todd, far surpassed any academic acumen I had ever displayed as an undergraduate student. Nevertheless, I was disappointed that the faculty had chosen to use a student. I was told that they chose a student because the experience would be enriching for all of their students. I will leave it to you the reader to draw your own conclusions.

After the debate (Todd was unprepared for my line of argumentation in the opening presentation and never really recovered), I spoke to Todd, not as an opponent but as a young man whom I respected and cared about. It is accurate to say that he believed that the faculty had done him a disservice.

I had a similar experience with a college professor at a liberal arts college near one of my pastorates. The gentleman was a professor of history, and he was stridently anti-Christian. Some of his students attended my church, and from time to time they would share with me some of the comments he made in his lectures. I wrote him a friendly letter and proposed a debate on the historicity of the resurrection of Jesus Christ or a related topic. After several weeks he wrote back and declined the offer. I was frustrated but not surprised by his answer. He said, "It is one thing to teach college freshmen; it is another thing to publicly debate." The idealist in me does not see much of a difference between teaching college students and debating in a public forum, but the realist in me got the message.

Now back to the debate that did take place. It happened in a lecture hall, and a fairly diverse group of people attended, including some members of my congregation, several philosophy students, and at least some of their professors. Of course, my brother-in-law came, as did some of his students. I was able to speak first, and my opening presentation went as follows:

> Good evening. I want to thank each of you for being here tonight. Whatever your convictions are about God, I hope you find this evening to be profitable. To the faculty of the philosophy department and the students of the philosophy club I want to give special thanks for your help in organizing and promoting tonight's debate. Most of all I want to thank my opponent [Mr. Todd Hayes*] for his kindness in our many communications. Why am I here tonight? (And I don't mean that in some deep philosophical sense.) Why do I want to participate in this debate? Like many of you, I have a thirst for knowledge, and having met with Todd I know that he will be very helpful as I seek to sharpen my thinking. But I can think of at least two motives more important than mere intellectual curiosity. First of all, I love God, and I want His name to be declared and glorified, for this is the highest purpose one can have in life.

Second, I care about each of you as individuals, and I certainly care about Todd. This is a practical application of my Christian worldview. The God Who created us can be personally known, and to know Him is to know the source of all life and truth.

In keeping with the stated purpose of this debate tonight, I would like to give you a reason for the hope that is within me. The question which has been posed is, "Does God exist?" i.e., Is there a God, and how can we know? I would like to begin my answer, which will be in the affirmative, by stating three basic factors.

First, we need to start with a definition. Since I am, by the grace of God, a Christian, I will be arguing for Christian theism. I cannot in good conscience argue for a concept of God which is not drawn from the Scriptures of the Old and New Testaments. The God of Christian theism is, by way of a simple working definition, the eternally self-existent creator of the universe, and He is both transcendent to it and immanent within it. God has made Himself known to us through the general revelation of the created order, through the special revelation of the Scriptures, and, most importantly, through the incarnation of the Son of God, Jesus Christ.

Second, I want you to know up front that my argument will not give a whole lot of consideration to the more popular traditional arguments for the existence of God, with which you might be familiar. By this I mean the arguments of men like Thomas Aquinas and those who follow in that tradition. What about the evidences presented by contemporary Christian apologists such as Josh McDowell and Gary Habermas, evidences which support the historical reliability of the Bible or the miraculous resurrection of Jesus Christ? What about evidences for the creation account of Genesis offered by scientists like Duane Gish? An abundance of such evidence is available, but I do not start with it because such an approach ignores that more fundamental clash of worldviews and the presuppositions upon which worldviews are built. A person's worldview will determine how he interprets evidence for or against the existence of God, so listing evidences is not the place to begin. And as far as the traditional arguments of Aquinas, I believe they fall short of proving the God of Christian theism. To reiterate my second preliminary then, I will not be stressing the more popular or well-known arguments and evidences for the God of Christian theism, for many of these arguments tend to put the cart before the horse.

I believe it is more constructive to argue for the existence of God by critiquing worldviews as a whole, rather than taking individual snippets of evidence, the interpretation of which is actually controlled by the worldview of the person looking at the evidence. This awareness of worldviews is the third controlling factor in my presentation tonight. I have a worldview, and so does Todd, and so do all of you. A person's worldview is the core set of beliefs and assumptions a person has by which he interprets all that he or she experiences in life. By focusing on worldviews it is my hope that we can avoid the O. J. Simpson/Duane Gish syndrome. Please allow me to explain what I mean by this.

For almost three years now we have been faced with the spectacle of the O. J. Simpson murder trial. One of the most interesting aspects of the whole process, at least to me, is to see how different people interpret the evidence based on their worldview, meaning their core beliefs or presuppositions. For instance, a significant segment of

the population believes that the criminal justice
system beginning with law enforcement is inherently racist, at least in Los Angeles. The distrust
created by racism (whether real or imagined)
causes some people to disregard the evidence
presented by the police. After all, the suspect is
a black man who has been far more successful in
life than many white people. Sadly, we can look
back in history and find examples of innocent
black men being victimized by a corrupt judicial
process. Consequently, the evidence presented
against Mr. Simpson is seen as tainted and therefore lacks any genuine persuasive power. There
would also be some people who are predisposed
to believe Mr. Simpson is guilty simply because
of the color of his skin, and such people are just
as unlikely to change their minds no matter how
much evidence the defense can present to clear
Simpson's name.

Someone might object to my illustration by
claiming that most people are not that captive to
their worldviews. I disagree. When the issue is
serious enough, worldviews are surrendered only
with the greatest of difficulty. Several weeks ago
a creation scientist by the name of Duane Gish
debated an evolutionist from Penn State Hazel-
ton right here on the campus of . . . University. I
would suggest to you that both men spoke past
each other and preached to their own respec-
tive choirs. For example, an atheistic evolutionist looks at the similarity between the DNA of a
chimpanzee and a man and says, "Aha, evidence
of a common ancestor." The special creationist
looks at the exact same evidence and says, "Aha,
evidence of a common creator." The conclusions
are completely opposite, yet they are perfectly
consistent with the worldview of each man, and
each man is frustrated by what he perceives to be

the close-mindedness of the other.

Well then, what should we do? If all the evidence I offer Todd will be unpersuasive because he filters it through an atheistic worldview, and if I reject Todd's arguments because of my theistic worldview, is there any hope of a truly meaningful debate tonight? In a sense we each wear worldview sunglasses. All that I see is tinted by the glasses I wear, and my brand of sunglasses is Christian theism. All that Todd sees is colored by his worldview sunglasses, glasses which are decidedly not Christian theistic. Someone might suggest that we should each take off our worldview glasses and in the spirit of neutrality examine the evidence objectively. In other words, let's simply follow the dictates of reason, and if theism isn't reasonable, let's reject it. Or if atheism isn't reasonable, we'll reject that.

I don't believe that such neutrality is possible, and it is naive to proceed as though it is. I do agree, however, that reason ought to be brought to bear on the question of God's existence. Guess what? If you agree with the approach that says reason is possible and essential, it shows that rather than being neutral or atheistic, you are thinking in accordance with the Christian worldview. As a matter of fact, my central argument tonight is that for Todd to use reason and the laws of logic, he must borrow from my worldview. The Christian worldview provides a basis for reason and logic; whereas, if atheism were true, there could be no such thing as reason or the laws of logic, not to mention laws of science and objective moral values. In a very real sense Todd lost tonight's debate the moment he decided to be a part of it.

What I am submitting for your consideration is what is known as the transcendental argument for the existence of God. For those interested in the history of this argument, there will be copies of a bibliography available after the debate. In general, the argument was most powerfully communicated by the late Dr. Greg Bahnsen, a student of Cornelius Van Til, who was, for many years, professor of apologetics at Westminster Theological Seminary in Philadelphia.

Basically, the transcendental argument for God is that He is the necessary precondition if there is to be any intelligibility of reason, the laws of logic, the laws of science, and objective moral values. Both my worldview and Todd's worldview make use of reason, logic, science, and ethics; on that I think we can agree. My contention is that my worldview can account for these things, while Todd's cannot. Thus atheism is internally incoherent and cannot account for human experiences; whereas, Christian theism is consistent. Thus my worldview sunglasses can be trusted, and Todd's cannot.

Consider the basic premise of atheism. If the universe is atheistic, it is nothing more than matter in motion. It is natural, not supernatural. It is wholly material in nature, with no immaterial entities. In other words, a naturally occurring material or physical universe does not allow for the existence of a supernatural, immaterial, or nonphysical God. Not only is there no currently existing microscope under which we can put a sample of God, no such microscope could ever be devised, for the very essence of God is outside of nature and matter. Scientists are fond of telling us that no supernatural explanations are permitted. To posit God as an explanation of phenomena which occurs in a natural, material universe is to make a non-statement which cannot explain anything.

The problem with the atheist's universe is that

it eliminates more than God; it also eliminates reason, the laws of logic, the laws of science, objective moral values, and any hope of an under- *morals* standing of the human mind which is not absurd. A universe which is strictly material in nature cannot account for any of these things. "But wait just a minute," someone might say, "atheists are committed to the use of reason, logic, science, and ethics. Many of the greatest scientific advances have come from atheists, and many atheists lead morally admirable lives, even surpassing some professing Christians I know."

Now, I certainly don't deny that atheists do all these things, but by their use of reason, logic, science, and ethics they are actually showing that in their hearts they know the God Who created them, for these things make sense in the Christian worldview but not in the atheist world. You see, in the Christian worldview there can be things such as universal abstract laws such as the laws of logic, which means that one truly can reason. In the Christian worldview there are immaterial realities, there are objective moral absolutes, there is a God Who orders the universe so that we can expect a uniformity of experience which provides the basis for making predictions, a linchpin of empirical science.

One way of summarizing the proof for the existence of God is by showing the impossibility of the contrary. If there is no God, we have no basis for believing there are such things as the laws of *materialism* logic, the uniformity of nature, objective moral values, or human minds which can genuinely discover truth. And if there is no basis for these things, why are we even here having this debate? It is because both Todd and I believe in logic, reason science, and ethics. But as I have stated, a universe which is only matter in motion cannot produce such realities. We are left with the ironic situation of atheists borrowing from the Christian worldview and then turning around and denying the validity of that worldview.

If you are not familiar with the transcendental argument for the existence of God, some of my assertions tonight might strike you as odd, so perhaps in the next segment we can explore what is meant by "reason," "the laws of logic," and "the human mind," and why atheism cannot account for such things. For now, I will take my last few minutes to consider the inadequacies of atheism in the realm of objective moral values.

The morning after the creation-evolution debate, I had breakfast with Todd, and he expressed irritation with what he perceived to be a mishandling of quotes or citations by Dr. Gish. Clearly, Todd believed that Dr. Gish had some sort of obligation to be honest and truthful. As a side note, I want to say that I think Dr. Gish shares this sense of obligation. I also think most, if not all, of you here tonight came with the expectation that both Todd and I would be honest in our argumentation. I'm sure Todd expects me to be honest, and would see [honesty] as obligatory in a debate such as this. We both agreed several weeks ago on some parameters of tonight's debate, and Todd would be justified in viewing me as being under ethical obligation to keep my word—justified, that is, if he borrows from my worldview. In the Christian worldview, when a person gives his word, he is obligated to keep it. To be a liar is not simply impolite; it is genuinely wrong. In an atheist world there can be no such thing as universal objective moral absolutes by which I can be judged to be in the wrong, no matter how egregious my lies.

If I engage in a series of lies here tonight, I believe Todd has just two logical responses available to him. He can (a) justly condemn my behavior by holding me to an objective universal standard. Of course, to do this he will need to use my world-view, the very thing he denies.

Or he must (b) protect atheism by denying the existence of objective universal standards. But not only will this render him unable to condemn my lying, the absence of objective universal moral laws reduces Todd to silence in response to the atrocities of Hitler and Stalin, as well. If someone objects by saying my argument is simply inflammatory, I would have to take such a response as a failure to deal with the logic of my challenge.

Aldous Huxley rejected Christian theism and its moral absolutes. When he worked this out in his personal philosophy, he had this to say: "I had motives for not wanting the world to have a meaning; consequently I assumed that it had none, and was able without any difficulty to find satisfying reasons for this assumption. The philosopher who finds no meaning in the world is not concerned exclusively with a problem in pure metaphysics, he is also concerned to prove that there is no valid reason why he personally should not do as he wants to do, or why his friends should not seize political power and govern in the way that they find most advantageous to themselves. . . . For myself, the philosophy of meaninglessness was essentially an instrument of liberation, sexual and political."

If you don't like what Huxley is saying and wish to reject it, you must first reject atheism, for although many atheists may personally dislike Huxley's philosophy, atheism provides no objective means for condemning it. This dilemma is painfully obvious in the *Second Humanist Manifesto* of 1973. The *Manifesto* is openly opposed to Christian theism yet would also reject Huxley's version of ethics. The *Manifesto* says,

"We affirm that moral values derive their source from human experience. Ethics is autonomous and situational, needing no theological or ideological sanction. Ethics stems from human needs and interests. To deny this distorts the whole basis of life."

Further on in the *Manifesto* is a treatment of human sexuality, which includes these propositions:

"In the area of sexuality, we believe that intolerant attitudes, often cultivated by orthodox religions and puritanical cultures, unduly repress sexual conduct. . . . While we do not approve of exploitive, denigrating forms of sexual expression, neither do we wish to prohibit, by law or social sanction, sexual behavior between consenting adults. The many varieties of sexual exploration should not in themselves be considered evil. Without countenancing mindless permissiveness or unbridled promiscuity, a civilized society should be a tolerant one. Short of harming others or compelling them to do likewise, individuals should be permitted to express the sexual proclivities and pursue their life-styles as they desire. We wish to cultivate the development of a responsible attitude toward sexuality, in which humans are not exploited as sexual objects, and in which intimacy, sensitivity, respect, and honesty in interpersonal relations are encouraged."

Did you catch the glaring contradiction? The *Manifesto* denies all grounds for moral absolutes by embracing situational ethics, yet [it] then turns around and establishes its own moral standards. It rejects the restrictions orthodox religion places on sexual conduct as being "unduly repressive." It then turns around and places its own limits on sexual behavior promoting, "The development of

a responsible attitude toward sexuality in which
humans are not exploited as sexual objects, and in
which intimacy, sensitivity, respect and honesty in
interpersonal relations are encouraged."

But why in an atheist universe do I have to
accept those limits? What if I find it personally
satisfying to be exploitive, and I need to shun intimacy, sensitivity, respect, and honesty? There are
no objective universal moral absolutes in an atheist world. The humanists who signed the *Manifesto* might not like my behavior, but ultimately
their standards are merely arbitrary, and I am not
bound to them.

My question to Todd at this point would be,
"Which atheistic approach to ethics will you
take?" My contention is that Huxley's is consistent with atheistic presuppositions, while the
Manifesto's is not. If you subscribe to something
like the *Manifesto,* you need to explain how this
is anything other than arbitrary, subjective, and
conventional. In other words, how can anyone
else be seen as being morally obligated to agree
with your subjective standards? If your standards
are objective and universal, how is this possible in
an atheist universe? If you choose something akin
to Huxley, are you willing to let Hitler and Stalin
practice it? If Hitler was truly morally wrong, tell
us how an atheistic worldview can establish his
guilt.

And if you concede Huxley's point and admit
you have no objective grounds for condemning
Hitler, you will still need to explain how an atheist
world can account for other laws outside of ethics,
such as the laws of logic by which you are debating tonight. And so I want to again insist that atheism cannot even account for tonight's debate. To
carry on with the debate is an implicit acknowl-
edgment of Christian theism. For by appealing to

reason, the laws of logic, and objective moral standards, we are appealing to standards which make sense in the Christian worldview; yet these standards cannot be accounted for within a universe that is merely matter in motion.

I have heard many atheistic arguments, and some of them are quite complex and difficult for me to understand. I freely admit that I came here tonight knowing that my opponent, who is extremely intelligent, might have an argument with which I am unfamiliar or incapable of comprehending without further study. However, whatever argument he uses, it will be something he has devised by the use of reason. Is reason material? I've never seen it, tasted it, smelled it, or touched it. If it is immaterial in nature, how can one account for it in a materialist universe? Once again, I believe that Todd will be depending on the Christian worldview which can make sense of reason, even as he argues against my worldview. If the debate goes poorly for me and I pull out a gun and shoot Todd, would I be guilty of something genuinely immoral, or have I merely acted on my personal brand of situational ethics?

As Dr. Greg Bahnsen argued so persuasively, "The proof of the Christian position is that unless its truth is presupposed, there is no possibility of proving anything at all." Is there a faith commitment on the part of the Christian? Absolutely. But what also ought to be clear, although it is usu- ally left unchallenged, is that the atheist also has faith commitments, and when I compare the two worldviews, I am forced to confess that I simply don't have enough faith to be an atheist. Thank you.

Name has been changed.

APPENDIX D

POSTMODERNISM

NOT many years ago the term "postmodernism" was unfamiliar to most people. Today many people have at least heard of the term. Still, it is a word that needs explanation because being familiar with the term does not necessarily mean someone can define it. Whether Christians understand postmodernism or not, it must not be ignored. It is rapidly becoming the giant in the neighborhood of worldviews. Its influences can be subtle, and it has already worked its way into churches. Christians who are committed to sharing and defending the gospel need to learn what postmodernism is, what drives it, and how we can communicate with men and women who have come under its influence.

Nailing Jell-O to the Wall

Someone has said that defining postmodernism is about as easy as nailing Jell-O to the wall. Postmodernism doesn't easily lend itself to definition, and some would say that the moment you attempt to define it, you reveal your inability to understand it. Sound confusing? Welcome to postmodernism. In many ways postmodernism is a rejection of traditional categories of reason and logic. Because of postmodernism's rejection of established laws of logic and rationalism, some Christians believe that rational apologetics itself is becoming obsolete. I believe the exact opposite, but more on that later. For now let's tackle the difficult task of defining postmodernism.

Modernism

"Postmodernism" is a broad term that refers to a worldview that is currently replacing modernism, thus the prefix "post," meaning "after." For the last few centuries in Western civilization, the prevailing worldview has been what is called modernism. At the risk of oversimplification, modernism is a worldview that grew out of the Enlightenment of the 1700s. The Enlightenment replaced what it perceived were the superstitions of religion and created a new object of faith: the scientific method and reason. Modernism dismissed historic Christianity as being prescientific or nonscientific, and therefore obsolete.[1] Modernism advocates universal laws and principles of truth. However, modernists do not find their universals through the agency of God, Who supernaturally reveals truth. For modernists, truth is discovered through the use of reason, logic, and the scientific method. Appeals to God or revelation are not permitted. In general, modernism is a worldview that has confidence in the human ability to discover truth free of any dependence upon a god.

After Modernism

Postmodernism has a radically different approach to knowledge. Postmodernism is highly individualistic and subjective. Thus, according to it, what is true for you does not have to be true for me. What is moral for you may not be moral for me. Truth claims are suspect if not outright offensive. Each person's view of truth is at the mercy of his own unique circumstances and subculture. Postmodernists believe that each individual constructs or experiences the world in his own individual mind and that this individuality negates the possibility of universal, objective truth. Consistent postmodernists seek to resist being defined by the community through its rules and expectations. Postmodernists are their own moral universe unto themselves. Relativism reigns supreme.

Another way of understanding postmodernism is to think of it as being a mood or an intuitive way of perceiving things. Therefore, it is not interested in a distinct set of doctrines. A distinct set of doctrines would too closely resemble the uniformity and universality of modernism. Postmodernism simply won't accept a single view of anything. Consequently, modernism must go. Does this sound like pluralism? Yes! Pluralism and tolerance toward all worldviews is essential in postmodernism. This is why historic Christianity with its exclusive truth claims is just as unwelcome as modernism. (Yes, this is a contradiction.)

Symptoms of Postmodernism

Good Guys Wear White Hats

Sometimes it is easier to explain postmodernism by giving illustrations of it. Postmodernism's fingerprints are easily seen in media, such as music and movies. In the 1940s the typical cowboy or Western film usually had a consistent theme. The good guy wore a white hat and followed the rules, even if doing so required sacrifice. The bad guy wore a black hat and broke the rules. This theme began to change in the 1960s. If you study Westerns of that era, you will notice that the good guys no longer fit the traditional norms of behavior. The good guys sometimes wore black, repudiated the law, and had no interest but self-interest. The films still portrayed these people in a sympathetic manner, yet their worldview was contrary to that in the previous generation of Western heroes.

Sports Team or Superstar?

I believe one can see the influence of postmodernism in sports. It wasn't too long ago that team sports such as football were built around the concept of conformity, uniformity, and the minimizing of self. These standards were packaged under the banner of sportsmanship. What do you observe today when you watch an NFL game? The focus is now on the individual within the game. Although it is impossible to escape the necessity of functioning like a team, there has been a fundamental shift in the focal point. Many have rejected traditional concepts of sportsmanship. Interestingly, a term has been coined to identify the coaches, athletes, and fans who cling to the traditional approach to sports: "old school." What does that tell you about the radical change in Western culture?

If you ever get an opportunity to watch the old football movie *Knute Rockne, All American* (1940, starring Ronald Reagan and Pat O'Brien), you will see firsthand how out of step the worldview in that film seems with our culture. Not surprisingly, many young people today, having grown up in a postmodernist world, are gravitating toward nontraditional sports that stress the individual and nonconformity. These sports, even when they become competitive, lack the formalized structure of the older sports.

Serving Up Postmodernism

By the time most students graduate from high school, they have already been immersed in postmodernism. Unless they attend a distinctly Christian college or university, they will find that from their first day as college students, postmodernism will be an omnipresent part of their college experience. Postmodernism has brought about a major shift in the teaching of almost every subject including history, science, sociology, and the arts.

Language

Another symptom of postmodernism can be seen by its impact on conversational language. Have you ever noticed how the vast majority of people say "I feel" rather than "I think" when stating an opinion? Even highly educated people speaking on highly technical subjects often tell us how they feel rather than what they think!

good point

In Church

If postmodernism were to infiltrate churches, where would its influence be seen? The record is already clear. Polls taken within evangelicalism suggest that as many as 40 percent of professing evangelical Christians think that other religions are valid paths to God (contrary to John 14:6; Acts 4:12; Galatians 1:6–10). As many as 50 percent think that there are no moral absolutes. These beliefs are thoroughly contradicted by the Bible, but they are perfectly consistent with postmodernism.

Another area where churches exhibit postmodernist influence is music. The hymns that were written 150 years ago tended to stress theological and doctrinal content. Some deep theology could be learned just by singing hymns. Much of today's contemporary religious music minimizes doctrinal content and replaces it with the theme of personal relationship. It uses repetitiveness intended to create an emotional response. Unfortunately, many contemporary songwriters are unaware of how postmodernism has influenced their thinking, and they unwittingly undermine the importance of a theologically informed community of believers.

It is not just songwriters who are minimizing theology. Some influential authors have written books that encourage Christians to think in new categories that, rather than offering a Biblical critique of postmodernism, seek to embrace it. Christianity must always be willing to critique itself. But what if the result of the critique is that a new kind of Christianity emerges, a Christianity that dumbs down propositional truth and excuses this new form

Do we do well to embrace modernism or postmodernism? Of course (yesterday) postmodernism.

as a celebration of mystery? The result would not be the triumph of relevant Christianity over irrelevant vestiges of modernism. If churches embrace postmodernism, the move simply guarantees their irrelevance.

Reaching Postmodernists

There is a sense, however, in which postmodernism has done some favors for Christianity. The anti-supernaturalism of modernism and the unquestioned confidence in autonomous human reason have been undermined by postmodernism. In some ways postmodernism is correcting the swing of the cultural pendulum away from the extreme to which modernism had taken it. Of course, a cure can be as bad as the disease, and in this case postmodernism has taken the pendulum to an opposite extreme, which is just as misguided and destructive.

How can Christianity effectively communicate with postmodernists without compromising its message? Is it even possible to use apologetics when speaking to a worldview that says "everyone's truth is different"? Christians need to be prepared to interact with individuals who, rather than being open to logical critique, despise the idea of logical critique as being a form of oppression, bigotry, and intolerance. In this atmosphere, apologetical methods that seemed so promising in the twentieth century appear to be impotent in the twenty-first century.

Postmodernists are skeptical about historical truth claims. They view the record of history as being hopelessly prejudiced by those who wrote it. This view will certainly make our appeals to historical facts suspect, if not outright superfluous.

Postmodernists are skeptical about the interpretation of evidence. Objectivity and neutrality do not exist. Everything is so highly individualized that there is little value in critiquing evidence. "How you choose to view the evidence is true for you, but I have a different truth." (Please note that the Biblical portrayal of sinful humanity is similar to postmodernism in its rejection of the possibility of neutrality. Our mutual rejection of some of the presuppositions of modernism can be a point of contact between Christians and postmodernists.)

The Truth Surpasses Postmodernism

Since postmodernism frowns on exclusive truth claims (especially in religion), is skeptical of logic, and embraces relativism, it would seem that apologetics, including ATW, will be fruitless. Nevertheless, Christians are aware of other factors that put things in a different light and preserve our commitment to apologetics.

First, man cannot escape the way God has made him and the nature of life itself. Consider once again the ramifications of passages such as Romans 1:18–21 and 2:14 and 15. Embracing a postmodern worldview might dampen the volume, but it cannot silence the testimony of God.

Furthermore, the nature of the reality in which we all live compels us to use logic every day. Consider the following proposition: "To get to the pizza shop, turn right at the second traffic light and drive exactly one mile." I can make that statement to a postmodernist, a modernist, an atheist, a Christian, a Muslim, and a Hindu, and we will all understand what it means. Language functions in a way experienced by all, no matter what various philosophers claim. One of the traits of all mankind is the ability to give and receive information by using language.[2] This ability is a gift of God.

What does this ability mean? For one thing, it calls into question whether knowledge is as individualistic as postmodernism claims. Maybe the prospect that there are knowable universals is not as far-fetched as some claim. The postmodernist may not like the same toppings on his pizza that I like on mine, but we can both agree on where the pizzeria is located and how much the Tuesday dinner special will cost. We live in the same world, and our lives are sustained by the same God. The postmodernist makes use of God-given abilities every day. He might not acknowledge their Source, but that is to be expected of any sinner. Again, we can find common ground for the communication of the gospel because postmodernists are not as nearly opposed to propositional truth as they think they are.

Finally, the advent of postmodernism has alerted many Christian apologists to the need for building personal and compassionate relationships with non-Christians. Although this need is nothing new, it is coming to the forefront of apologetics. Perhaps no testimony of the truthfulness of the Christian worldview is more powerful in the postmodern world than the love of Jesus Christ lived out and reflected in the lives of His followers.[3]

Notes

1. During the nineteenth and early twentieth centuries a great battle occurred within American Protestant Christianity. Church historians call it the modernist-fundamentalist controversy. As philosophical modernism became a dominant worldview, many within Protestant Christianity sought to reconcile Christianity with the truth claims of modernism. Since modernism was anti-supernaturalistic, Christianity was redefined to minimize its supernaturalistic beliefs. Some of the changes included a denial of the deity of Jesus Christ, a denial of His bodily resurrection from the dead, a denial of the inerrancy of the Bible, and a rejection of most of the Biblical accounts of miracles. The theories of Darwin and the claims of higher criticism were embraced, thereby requiring a reinterpretation of Genesis.

What emerged was a new form of Christianity called "modernism" or "liberalism." The brilliant Princeton theologian J. Gresham Machen wrote a classic treatment of the issue, *Christianity and Liberalism*, and made a compelling argument that the new form of "Christianity" was actually a new religion and that it was intellectually dishonest for it to retain the name "Christian."

Christians who opposed the redefining of Christianity fought to maintain the historic truths or fundamentals of Biblical Christianity. The natural results of championing the fundamentals led to this movement being called "fundamentalism." Thus the modernist-fundamentalist controversy was a clash within Christianity having to do with how Christianity would respond to philosophical modernism. (Note: Labels can become confusing. When I say "philosophical modernism," I am talking about the worldview in general. The segment of Christianity that accommodated and embraced philosophical modernism was religious modernism. It is this second use of the term "modernism," the religious modernism, that we refer to when we speak of the modernist-fundamentalist controversy.)

Because religious modernism rejected the authority of the Bible, it has not been difficult for many modernist churches to simply adopt postmodernism in recent years. Whether one is a modernist or a post-modernist, the common theme is *homo mensura*: man is the measure of all things. The fifth encounter, "The Liberal 'Christian'" (p. 121), between Sean and Glenn demonstrates how easily liberal Christianity can drift back and forth between modernism and postmodernism.

2. The nature of language and its limitations is a never-ending topic for debate among philosophers. Often the result of these academic debates is more smoke than light. This book has not been written to delve into the complexities of the debate. The position of ATW is that although language is full of pitfalls, it is still a God-given platform for knowing and communicating absolute truth. Of course, the gifts God gives are perfect. The problem is with the sinfulness of finite creatures. Postmodernism views language differently than does modernism or Christianity. Like everything else, language for the postmodernist is rooted in individualism. It can be manipulated to create one's own reality. Need an example? Try this: gay marriage. By almost every previously recognized standard of language and logic, gay marriage would have been considered an oxymoron, two words that ought not be used together (such as jumbo shrimp!). Marriage is the union between a man and a woman that makes them husband and wife. The postmodernist will not accept this sort of fixed, universal meaning.

3. Some observers have suggested that postmodernism is already a worldview in decline. The inability of a true postmodernist to

consistently condemn the terrorist acts of September 11 has caused it to lose its appeal to many who had previously celebrated it. Would it not be a sad irony if the secular world outgrew postmodernism, just at the time some within the church called for us to embrace it in the name of being relevant?

APPENDIX E

THE CENTRALITY OF LOGIC

L OGIC matters to God. It is how He thinks and how He requires Christians to think (Isa. 1:18). When Christians disparage the importance of logic, they are not demonstrating Biblical thinking and are not honoring God. When Christians construct arguments through the use of faulty logic, God is not honored. Of all people, Christians should reject faulty arguments no matter how much the conclusions appeal to them. The God of truth is not served by irrationalism.

In the foreword to Gordon Clark's book *Logic*, John Robbins wrote:

> Strictly speaking, there is no "mere human logic,"
> as contrasted with a divine logic. The Logic of
> God lights every man; human logic is the image
> of God. God and man think the same way, not
> exactly the same thoughts since man is sinful and
> God is holy. But both God and man think that two

plus two equals four, and that A cannot be non-A.
Both God and Christians think that only the sub-
stitutionary death of Christ can merit a sinner's
entrance into Heaven. The laws of logic are the
way God thinks. He makes no mistakes, draws no
unwarranted conclusions, constructs no invalid
arguments. We do, and that is one of the reasons
why we are commanded by the apostle Paul to
bring all our thoughts into captivity to Christ
(2 Corinthians 10:5). We ought to think as Christ
does—logically.[1]

The Bible regularly invites its readers to draw proper conclusions from its stated propositions. This is the heart and soul of
logic. Paul's letter to the Romans is a classic example of logical
argumentation. Whenever Paul used the word "therefore," he
was challenging the reader to infer the truth from what he had
already stated. Paul also repudiated the tendency of people to
draw false conclusions based on this misuse of logic (see 6:1;
9:14, 18, 19, 30). God expects Christians to reason properly (Luke
24:25-27). I am alarmed when I hear Christian teachers dismiss
logic as an obstacle to knowing God or genuine spirituality.

The ATW method makes use of logic. At times it might appear that in the encounters the Christians are trusting logic more
than the Scriptures. In truth, however, they are using logic in a
manner that is consistent with the Scriptures (Prov. 26:4, 5) and
with the implicit recognition (not always explicitly stated) that
logic testifies of the Creator Who is foundational to logic itself. An
accurate analysis of the nature of logic and its use in argument
compels us to submit to Scripture if logic is to have any reliable
justification. And if logic cannot be justified, we are all in trouble,
for once we surrender the law of contradiction, human existence
becomes unable to be defended.

At the risk of being redundant, I want to again stress that the
use of logic in the encounter section (part 2) is not for granting

unbelievers intellectual autonomy. Nor does logic enable man to arrive at spiritual truth unaided by God or the Bible. The Christians in the encounters all use logic as being a point of contact or common ground with the unbelievers. Logic is an inescapable element of human existence. Even the most irrational person still uses logic in a myriad of ways every day of his life. The key is that it is illogical to be logical apart from submitting to the God Who has created and ordered the universe.

In this sense, there are no atheists. All men live as though they know God, even though they suppress that knowledge and outwardly profess atheism. Short of being born again, they cannot escape the impact of sin on their moral ability to use logic consistently. But short of death they cannot escape tipping their hands and revealing the image of God in which they were made and against which they are in rebellion.

The same holds true for postmodernists. Many people today see no use for logic, and they openly revile it. The colossal shift toward postmodernism in recent years means that Christians will often find people who have no interest in logical critiques of any worldview. I believe the same dynamic that says, "There are no true atheists" can also lead us to conclude that there are no true postmodernists. Like atheists, postmodernists can mentally suppress the truth of Christianity, but they cannot ultimately escape the way God has made them and the way He has made the universe. Everyone depends on logic, but not everyone realizes it or admits it.

Notes

1. Gordon Clark, *Logic* (Unicoi, TN: Trinity Foundation, 1985), xi.

ETHICS AS
A FORMAL
DISCIPLINE

EVERYONE is interested in ethics, at least on the practical level of daily life. But as a formal academic discipline, the study of ethics demands considerable attention from philosophers and theologians. Christian readers are encouraged to actively study in this field, especially considering the ever-increasing confusion over ethics in our secular society.

At the risk of oversimplification, ethics can be divided in a couple of basic ways. First, one can say that ethics is either discovered or invented. "Discovered" implies a source outside man and often leads to the discussion of God. "Invented" implies that men must devise their own systems of ethics based on their own judgment and experiences.

Discovered Ethics

If ethics are discovered, the discussion will often lead to the question, Who speaks for God? or To whom has God spoken? The possibility of discovering a rudimentary system of ethics by looking inward exists, because God has given man an innate awareness of God's ethical demands (Rom. 2:14, 15). The original source of these ethics is still external to man. The conscience is hampered by the sin nature. The only completely reliable ethics are those revealed by God in His Word (Ps. 119:1–11).

Invented Ethics

If ethics are invented, the discussion will often lead to the question, What do I want my ethics to be? There are two basic yet related systems at this level.

First, there is egoism, an individualistic approach that says, "My ethics will be that which will best serve my interests." (This approach does not exclude the possibility of trying to please others, for a person may find that pleasing others is advantageous.)

A second option is utilitarianism. Utilitarians believe that ethics should be based on finding "the greatest good for the greatest number." John Stuart Mill is considered the father of utilitarianism. He believed that calculations could be made to determine which courses of action would produce pleasure for the greatest number of people.

The problem with inventing ethics is that one cannot escape relativism. To make things worse, how does anyone truly know what "the good" is? And since man is not omniscient, how can he truly predict the outcome of his actions? And since he cannot know the outcome, how can he know if what he has chosen is actually good?

Means and Ends

A second useful division in the study of ethics is the distinction between means and ends. Which is the final standard? Some would say, "It's not whether you win or lose, but how you play the game." These people find ultimacy in the rules. The technical term for this division is deontological ethics.

Others would argue that the final standard is getting good results: "The end justifies the means." This view is known as teleological ethics, for the focus is on the end (the *telos*) of the action. Thus winning isn't everything; it's the only thing.

Biblical ethics has room for both caring deeply about the rules and for being sensitive to the human factor and the results of our rule-keeping. The fact that Christians must operate in a fallen world means they will face some perplexing ethical questions. (Should I lie to protect my children from a potential murderer?) But those who reject God have no possibility of devising an ethical system that is not inherently flawed. Several of the encounters in this book reflect this weakness in the non-Christian worldviews. Non-Christian ethicists have devised complex systems, and Christians should study well enough to be familiar with them. Nevertheless, even the most complex man-made system can be reduced to the inevitable plague of relativism or false religions.

Ethics Shift

I believe that a major shift in Western culture has taken place in the last fifty years. Millions of people are seeking to invent their own ethics. These people do not believe there is a binding, authoritative source of ethics from a source external to man. Advocacy groups such as the American Civil Liberties Union (ACLU) fight to have displays of the Ten Commandments removed from government buildings. Yet the record of history is clear. American law was founded upon a belief that law is rooted in a Supreme Creator. Law and ethics are now seen by millions as being rooted in what man can devise unaided by God.

The magnitude of this shift can be felt every day. The consequences of this shift are alarming. Nevertheless, a proper view of the Bible and history (see chapter 4, "The 'Blessing' of Immoral-ity") should encourage Christians to see the wonderful oppor-tunity the current cultural climate is providing for sharing the gospel. The encounters sections reflect this outlook.

GLOSSARY

Absolutism—Advocacy of a rule by absolute standards or principles.

Acumen—Keenness and depth of perception, discernment, or discrimination especially in practical matters.

Anarchy—A state of lawlessness or political disorder due to the absence of governmental authority; the absence or denial of any authority or established order.

Animate—Possessing or characterized by life; alive.

Apologetics—The study of the defense of the Christian faith.

Arbitrary—Based on or determined by individual preference or convenience rather than by necessity or the intrinsic nature of something.

Atypical—Not typical; irregular; unusual.

Autonomy—Self-law or self-rule.

Benevolent—Loving.

The Christ—Messiah.

Cogent—Appealing forcibly to the mind or reason; convincing; pertinent; relevant.

Contradictory—Mutually exclusive.

Deism—A system of thought advocating natural religion, emphasizing morality, and in the eighteenth century denying the interference of the Creator with the laws of the universe.

Deontolgocial—Having to do with the study of moral obligation.

Dred Scott—Scott was a slave who traveled in and out of "free" states with his owner, an army doctor. After the doctor died, Scott offered to pay for his and his wife's freedom, but the doctor's widow and brother (executor of the estate) refused the offer. When the widow rented Scott to someone else, Scott sued for his and his wife's freedom. The case eventually went to the Supreme Court, where Scott lost.

Emperor without clothes—This phrase indirectly refers to a story written by Hans Christian Andersen, "The Emperor's New Suit" (1837). Two swindlers tell the emperor that they've made him a new suit out of special cloth. They claim that clothes made of their material possess the wonderful quality of being invisible to anyone who is unfit for office or who is unpardonably stupid. Neither the emperor, his court, or his subjects are willing to say anything about his nonexistent new suit for fear of being considered unfit or stupid. Eventually a child reveals what all the people know but are too afraid to admit: the emperor is not wearing any clothes.

Epistemology—The study or a theory of the nature and grounds of knowledge especially with reference to its limits and validity.

Faith—(1) The exercise of obedience in deference to someone or something apart from oneself; (2) a set of beliefs or doctrine.

Fideism—Reliance on faith rather than reason in pursuit of religious truth.

Germane—Being at once relevant and appropriate.

Immanent—Indwelling; inherent; being within the limits of possible experience or knowledge.

Imperative—Something that is a command, order, rule, guide; an obligatory act or duty.

Inanimate—Not endowed with life or spirit.

Incoherence—The state of lacking orderly continuity, arrangement, or relevance; the state of being inconsistent.

Intellectual autonomy—The propensity of humans to set themselves up as the highest or final authority when it comes to the question of truth.

Karma—According to Hinduism and Buddhism, it is the force generated by a person's actions. Supposedly it perpetuates migration of a soul from one body to another and determines the quality of the next life.

Law of Contradiction—Two opposite propositions cannot both be true at the same time and in the same sense.

Legal positivism—Legal positivism implies that law can be separated from ethics.

Linchpin—One that serves to hold together parts or elements that exist or function as a unit.

Litmus test—A test in which a single factor (e.g., an attitude, event, or fact) is decisive.

Maya—Illusion.

Monism—A view that there is only one kind of ultimate substance; the view that reality is an undivided organic whole with no independent parts.

Natural man—A person who is unsaved.

Nirvana—The final state of bliss that goes beyond suffering, karma, and samsara (the indefinitely repeated cycles of birth, misery, and death supposedly caused by karma). Nirvana is sought especially in Buddhism through the extinction of desire and individual consciousness.

Neo-pagan—A person who practices a contemporary form of paganism (e.g., Wiccan).

Nihilism—A doctrine or belief that conditions in the social organization are so bad that they make destruction desirable for its own sake, independent of any constructive program or possibility.

Nuremberg Laws—Three laws passed in Nuremberg, Germany, on September 15, 1935, by the Congress of the National Socialist Workers' Party (NAZI). The laws (1) spelled out the requirements for citizenship in the Third Reich, (2) attempted to secure the purity of German blood and German honor, and (3) explained the Jews' position in the Third Reich. The Third Reich was Germany and some surrounding countries with German ethnic populations under Nazi control.

Omnipotent—All-powerful.

Omniscient—Knowing all.

Pantheism—A doctrine that equates God with the forces and laws of the universe; the worship of all gods of different creeds, cults, or peoples indifferently.

Pluralism—A theory that there are more than one or more than two kinds of ultimate reality; also a theory that reality is composed of a plurality of beings.

Postmodernism—A theory that involves a radical reappraisal of modern assumptions about culture, identity, history, or language. Also see appendix D (p. 239).

Pragmatism—An American movement in philosophy marked by the doctrines that the meaning of conceptions is to be sought in their practical bearings, that the function of thought is to guide action, and that truth is preeminently to be tested by the practical consequences of belief.

Pre-evangelism—Laying common ground with unbelievers.

Preliminary (n.)—Something that precedes or is introductory or preparatory.

Premise—Something assumed or taken for granted.

Presupposition—A primary or foundational belief through which all other information is interpreted.

Presuppositionalism—For a definition and discussion, see appendix B (p. 217).

Relative—Not absolute or independent.

Relativism—A theory that knowledge is relative to the limited nature of the mind and the conditions of knowing; also, a view that ethical truths depend on the individuals and groups holding them.

Supernaturalist—Characterized by belief in a supernatural power and order of existence.

Teleological—Exhibiting or relating to design or purpose especially in nature.

Theodicy—A justification of the ways of God.

Universal (adj.)—Including or covering all without limit or exception; present or occurring everywhere; existent or operative everywhere or under all conditions.

Universal (n.)—A behavior pattern or institution (e.g., the family) existing in all cultures.

Vegan—A strict vegetarian who consumes no animal food or dairy products; one who abstains from using animal products (e.g., leather).

Wicca—A religion influenced by pre-Christian beliefs and practices of Western Europe. It affirms the existence of supernatural power (e.g., magic) and of both male and female deities who belong in nature. It emphasizes ritual observance of seasonal and life cycles.

Worldview—A person's core beliefs, which provide him with a "lens" through which he sees and interprets the world and his place in it. (See "General Description" in appendix A, pp. 209 ff.)

RECOMMENDED READING

O N THE bookshelves in my office are several hundred books on apologetics, theology, and philosophy. All of them have value and have helped shape my thinking. Many of the authors, including the apologists, have viewpoints that differ from mine on various points. They have still been my teachers, and I am grateful for them. But for the purpose of a recommended reading list, I wanted to present a relatively small number of works. Since *Ask Them Why* is a work modest in size and scope, I believe it is appropriate to keep the reading list small. These books are superior to anything I could ever write, though they and their authors may not be wholly endorsed by the publisher of my work, and I urge the reader not to conclude that these authors would endorse ATW either.

Bahnsen, Greg L. *Always Ready: Directions for Defending the Faith.* Texarkana, AR: Covenant Media Foundation, 1996.

Bahnsen, Greg L., and Gordon Stein. *The Great Debate: Does God Exist?* 1985. Debate held at University of California, Irvine. Available on CD or mp3 from Covenant Media Foundation.

Beckwith, Francis J., and Gregory Koukle. *Relativism: Feet Firmly Planted in Mid-Air.* Grand Rapids: Baker Books, 1998.

Boa, Kenneth D. and Robert M. Bowman, Jr. *Faith Has Its Reasons: An Integrative Approach to Defending Christianity.* Colorado Springs: NavPress, 2001.

Bruce, F. F. *The Defense of the Gospel in the New Testament,* rev. ed. Leicester, England: InterVarsity Press, 1977.

Carson, D. A. *The Gagging of God: Christianity Confronts Pluralism.* Grand Rapids: Zondervan Publishing House, 1996.

Clark, Gordon H. *Religion, Reason and Revelation*, 2nd ed. Jefferson, MD: The Trinity Foundation, 1986.

Cowan, Stephen B., and Stanley N. Gundry, eds. *Counterpoints: Five Views on Apologetics.* Grand Rapids: Zondervan Publishing House, 2000.

Frame, John M. *Apologetics to the Glory of God: An Introduction.* Phillipsburg, NJ: Presbyterian and Reformed Publishing, 1994.

Geisler, Norman. *False Gods of Our Time: A Defense of the Christian Faith.* Eugene, OR: Harvest House Publishers, 1985.

Habermas, Gary R. *Ancient Evidence for the Life of Jesus: Historical Records of His Death and Resurrection.* Nashville: Thomas Nelson Inc., 1984.

Johnson, Phillip E. *Reason in the Balance: The Case against Naturalism in Science, Law, and Education.* Downers Grove, IL: InterVarsity Press, 1995.

Kreeft, Peter. *Socrates Meets Jesus: History's Greatest Questioner Confronts the Claims of Christ.* Downers Grove, IL: InterVarsity Press, 1987.

Mayers, Ronald B. *Both/And: A Balanced Apologetic.* Grand Rapids: Kregel Publications, 1996.

McDowell, Josh, and Don Stewart. *Handbook of Today's Religions: Understanding Secular Religions.* San Bernadino, CA: Here's Life Publishers, 1982.

Moreland, J. P. *Scaling the Secular City: A Defense of Christianity.* Grand Rapids: Baker Book House, 1987.

Nash, Ronald H. *Faith and Reason: Searching for a Rational Faith.* Grand Rapids: Academic Books/Zondervan, 1988.

Oliphant, K. Scott. *The Battle Belongs to the Lord: The Power of Scripture for Defending our Faith.* Phillipsburg, NJ: Presbyterian and Reformed Publishing.

Schaeffer, Francis A., and C. Everett Koop. *Whatever Happened to the Human Race?* Old Tappan, NJ: Revell, 1979.

Wilson, Douglas. *Persuasions: A Dream of Reason Meeting Unbelief.* Moscow, ID: Oakcross Publications, 1989.

Zacharias, Ravi: *A Shattered Visage: The Real Face of Atheism.* Brentwood, TN: Wolgemuth and Hyatt, Publishers, Inc., 2004.

SPECIAL THANKS

We express our appreciation to those involved in the audio production of the Ask Them Why *encounters.*

Director
Reba Hervas is president of Overshadowed Theatrical Productions, Itasca, Illinois. Learn more at www.overshadowedproductions.com.

Audio Engineer
Chris Brown is a digital media missionary with Gospel Literature Services. Learn more at www.glsonline.org.

Actors
Jordan Caterina

Peter Comps

Robert Cummings

Charles Hervas

Reba Hervas

Tracy Holloway

Dave Jaspers

Eleanor Kernitz

Breana Larsen

Michael Larsen

Matthew Lew

Mark Massaro

Michelle Plonk

Terry Powell

Paula Wiggins